Biography

Rick

Ross

Great Steps in Music and Business

Brandie L McFarlin

The contents of this book may not be copied, reproduced or transmitted without the express written permission of the author or publisher. Under no circumstances will the publisher or author be responsible or liable for any damages, compensation or monetary loss arising from the information contained in this book, whether directly or indirectly. .

Disclaimer Notice:

Although the author and publisher have made every effort to ensure the accuracy and completeness of the content, they do not, however, make any representations or warranties as to the accuracy, completeness, or reliability of the content. , suitability or availability of the information, products, services or related graphics contained in the book for any purpose. Readers are solely responsible for their use of the information contained in this book

Every effort has been made to make this book possible. If any omission or error has occurred unintentionally, the author and publisher will be happy to acknowledge it in upcoming versions.

Chapter 1

My grandfather was not a violent man or a civil rights activist. He was a family man, a farmer, and a quartet gospel singer at his church. But no one was going to take his babies away in the middle of the night. If a mob of Ku Klux Klansmen showed up at his house, he was going to bury at least a couple of them. That's what all those guns were for.

When my mother was nine years old, an electrical fire destroyed the Fieldses' family house. The incident prompted their relocation to Clarksdale, where Rosie Lee's parents—Claude and Amy McAfee, my great-grandparents—hosted them in their Barnes Avenue house until my grandparents could recover.

My grandfather had only completed eighth grade, but he refused to let that stop him. He was constantly looking for the next larger and better chance to support his increasing family. He didn't need a formal education to realise that sharecropping, as an American institution, was dying. Mechanical cotton pickers were replacing African plantation hands. As a result, he retired from his position as a tenant farmer and began working at Delta Packing Company in Clarksdale.

He worked there for a few years before moving on to the oil mill, where the pay was slightly higher. This enabled him to move his family out of his in-laws' house and onto their own down the street for $3,000. But Rosie Lee kept the kids coming, and it wasn't long before the oil mill was underpaying as well. The Fields family was going to require a larger home.

That's when my grandfather began driving the hour and a half up Highway 61 to work in Memphis, Tennessee. He started as a driver and then became a mechanic for Campbell Trucking Company. He advanced through the ranks, finally becoming their first black supervisor. A guinea pig for the company's initial attempts at racial integration.

He'd spend the week in Memphis, then return to Clarksdale on weekends. My mother would not leave his side. On Saturdays, he worked on neighbours' cars to make a little more money, and she would accompany him outside all day, collecting him whatever equipment he required and bringing him something refreshing to drink to combat the humid Mississippi heat. They spent their weekends bonding and catching up. My mother was reticent and shy, but she told her father everything that passed her mind. He was her best friend. She didn't open out to anyone else in that way, including her mother and younger siblings.

My grandfather bought an eleven-room brick home at 428 McKinley Street from a preacher in 1967, and the property is still in the family today. They maintained the house on Barnes Street and turned it into a tiny café. The café became Rosie Lee's livelihood. She'd work in the evenings, when people were leaving work and seeking somewhere to eat a hamburger, drink a beer or a pint of corn whiskey, and dance to music blasting from the Seeburg jukebox.

After graduating from high school in 1968, my mother attended Coahoma Junior College for a year before moving to Mississippi Valley State University, a black college in Leflore County. She graduated from the school's nursing program in 1971, having been as dedicated and diligent as she was bright. It was the first of several degrees she would obtain in the field of health sciences.

Mississippi Valley State was also where my mother met my father. He was not from the Delta. William Leonard Roberts, born on September 26, 1935, grew up in Lloyd, a small hamlet in North Florida located between Jefferson and Leon counties. He was the first child of William Roberts and Mabel Leonard Roberts. Mabel already had a son from her first marriage, my uncle May Williams. My father's parents had two more children a few years later: my aunt Carrie and my uncle Arthur. We call him Uncle Tudor.

In 1946, the Robertses relocated from Lloyd to central Florida and lived in Brewster, a mining community in Polk County. Brewster is no longer around. It's been a ghost town since the 1960s. However, it was formerly a profitable business town for American Cyanamid, whose primary commodity was phosphate. My grandfather found a job in the phosphate mines and worked there for over four decades until he retired.

William Roberts, like my grandfather on my mother's side, was an uneducated guy. He did, however, ensure that his children were present. He saw that guys who worked in the mines developed a variety of cancers—leukaemia, lymphoma, and mesothelioma—and he wanted his children to have the alternatives he did not. Getting an education was the ticket out of this radiation-contaminated village.

My father's nickname at home was "Tut," but at school and across the town, he was known as "Big Brewster." Everyone knew Big Brewster the Bruiser. He was the star defensive tackle for Union Academy's football team and a standout wrestler. The man was a stud. My mother claims my father and I have the same build. My sister swears that we walk the same manner.

After graduating from Union Academy in 1956, my father briefly attended Wiley College, a black school in Marshall, Texas. But his studies would be placed on hold. After his first semester, he was drafted into the US Army. He was deployed to Germany, where he served his first tour of duty on a helicopter crew guarding the Russian border. On his return, he resumed his studies at Florida A&M University in Tallahassee. But he was still in the reserves, and after a year at A&M, he was transferred back to Europe.

He somehow ended up in New York City after his years in the military. He spent his early twenties there, first as a computer programmer for IBM and later at Chemical Bank. My father was a tremendously educated person, particularly when it came to technology.

He received his bachelor's degree in business administration from Delaware State University in 1969. And that's when he left for Mississippi Valley State, where he accepted a position as the school's assistant union director.

Growing up, my father was regarded as a hometown hero. He was a popular guy who enjoyed having a good time, and he had a thing for the young coeds on Mississippi Valley State's campus. But when he pulled up to my mommy in his beige Buick Riviera and tried to talk to her, she refused. He was her type—smart, personable, and athletic—but she didn't want to date someone fifteen years her senior, particularly a school employee. This was frowned upon. Plus, she had a boyfriend at the time. Nathaniel Dorsey, a member of the school's football team, went on to play for the Pittsburgh Steelers.

My father may have figured that if this girl liked jocks, he'd ultimately get his opportunity. It took longer than intended, but he eventually wore her down. My mother had graduated and was working as a nurse at Taborian Hospital in Mound Bayou. My father had likewise left Mississippi Valley State to teach at Coahoma Community College in Clarksdale while pursuing his MBA at Delta State University. They did, however, belong to similar social circles and would occasionally cross paths. She had his phone number, and one night, when she needed a lift home from work, she called him.

That night, one thing led to another, and my mother was soon faced with a difficult dilemma. She still harboured affections for Nathaniel. But she had long ago promised herself that she would remain a virgin for her spouse. At the end of the day, she couldn't bring herself to breach her word. She broke up with Nathaniel and began a relationship with my father. To be honest, I think my mother is still wondering what might have happened with that other guy.

My parents married shortly thereafter in the Coahoma County courthouse, and my sister was born a year and a half later. Her full name is Tawanda Roberts, although she goes by her middle name inside the family. Renee.

My family decided to relocate to Miami after my father obtained a position as the business manager at Florida Memorial College in Miami Gardens. My mother had been pregnant again, so it was not the worst moment for her to be between jobs. With her nursing expertise, she was confident she would be able to find work and further her career in Miami.

However, unlike my father, she had never lived in a big city, so Miami was a big shift for her. She kept her emotions contained, but the transition was difficult for her. This was a country girl from Clarksdale, where there was a definite division of class and culture. She had spent the first twenty-five years of her life in a close-knit community with neighbours who had lived next to each other for generations and looked out for one another. She'd only ever spent time with other Southern black people, and now she was in a melting pot of Cubans, Haitians, Jamaicans, Bahamians, East Indians, and Trinidadians. Her new neighbours practised Haitian voodoo and

Santería. They would bring home goats to sacrifice in the backyard, then smear themselves with the blood after cutting off their heads.

She faced several forms of cultural shock. Driving in Miami was really overwhelming for her. Nobody had ever told her that avenues go north to south and streets run east to west. She avoided the expressway entirely. She developed agoraphobia and made few new pals. The local news bothered her, so she began praying more. These were some of the reasons why my mother opted to return home the week before I was born.

My parents' aspirations extended beyond the modest joys of Mississippi farm life. They knew there would be more and better chances in Miami. For themselves and their children. What they didn't realise was that they were on the verge of a brutal and horrible period in the city's history. A storm was coming. A lot of crap was going to go down.

Chapter 2

My parents rented a house in Hialeah, which is west of Miami, where I spent my first year. But I can't remember anything about that place. My first memories are from Carol City, near the corner of 183rd Street and 39th Court, where my parents purchased a little three-bedroom, two-bathroom home in the spring of 1977.

Aside from the seafoam-green paint job, my house resembled every other neighbourhood. Because of the hurricanes, all of Miami's inner city residences are built with the same materials: concrete, reinforced steel bars, and stormproof windows. Inside the house, everything was also concrete. The ceiling. The walls. The floors. South Florida is too hot for carpeting.

Behind my house were a number of housing projects. Two junkies lived in the bushes separating my garden from the apartments. Sometimes I'd watch them from my bedroom window. At night, I could only see the flicker of flame from when they lit up their crack. The cloud of smoke seemed different from when my father smoked his smokes. He smoked Benson & Hedges Menthol 100s. The crack smoke was thicker. It almost appeared blue.

One day, my curiosity got the best of me, and I decided to investigate the dope fiends' doghouse. I climbed through the bushes into their improvised home and glanced at the straight shooters, empty baggies, and cans of Schlitz malt liquor littered over the area. I could not believe that people lived like this.

Over the course of the 1970s, Miami's identity shifted from a calm vacation resort and retirement town to the American cocaine capital. Yayo had become the glamour drug of the rich and famous, and nowhere was the American thirst for powder more pronounced than in Miami.

As the blow industry exploded, rival factions of Colombians and Cubans began to clash. The "Cocaine Cowboys" era began on July 11, 1979, with a deadly shooting in broad daylight at the Dadeland Mall. Every day, more bodies were being found. The assassinations exposed the narco underworld that had taken control of the city.

The situation was no better on the other side of the law. Six months after the Dadeland shooting, five white Miami-Dade police officers were charged with fatally beating a thirty-three-year-old black man in Liberty City. His name was Arthur McDuffie.

On the night of December 21, 1979, McDuffie, an insurance salesman and former US Marine, ran a red light while riding a Kawasaki 900. When the police activated their sirens, he led them on a high-speed chase. It would take eight minutes before McDuffie gave up and pulled over at the intersection of North Miami Avenue and 38th Street. His submission earned him no leniency. Police surrounded him and used nightsticks to smash his brains in. The crackers cracked his skull open "like an egg," as the prosecutor later recounted. McDuffie died of his injuries four days later.

To conceal their murder, the police ran over McDuffie's bike and broke its glass gauges, making it appear that his death was the result of a traffic accident. It didn't take long for the county medical examiner to become real and call that bullshit.

When the cover-up failed and five officers were accused, their defence counsel transferred the trial from Miami to Tampa, where they were able to assemble an all-white jury. When pressed to explain her decision to move the trial, Miami-Dade Circuit Judge Lenore C. Nesbitt labelled the McDuffie case a "time bomb".

"I don't want to see it go off in my courtroom or in this community," she told me.

The trial lasted more than a month, but it only took the jury two and a half hours to acquit the police of all counts. In a community with a long history of racial tensions, notably black people's hatred of police enforcement and the criminal justice system, this was the final nail in the coffin. The verdict shattered Miami.

The judge was correct in her evaluation of the case, but she was mistaken to believe she could defuse this bomb. It wouldn't matter where this injustice occurred. Black Miami people were consumed with wrath and took to the streets. By sunset, their protestations had evolved into something uglier. Looting and riots.

For four days, inner-city Miami burned. By the time it was over, eighteen men and women had been slain, with hundreds injured. The city suffered $100 million in property damage, all of which occurred in its minority communities.

Even if the rioting did not spread to Carol City, the McDuffie case had a significant impact. I was only four years old at the time, so I don't have very vivid memories of what happened. But the riots—and those that occurred in Overtown years later—influenced how I came to perceive the world around me. It got ingrained in the minds of Miami's black community. People discussed it all the time. Even when they weren't discussing it, it hung in the air.

The racial riots occurred during the height of the Mariel boatlift, when Fidel Castro said that everyone who wanted to escape Cuba was welcome. Over the next six months, more than 125,000 Cuban immigrants landed in Miami, with 85,000 arriving in the same month as the riots. The influx of Cubans coincided with another wave of Haitian immigration to Miami. Throughout the 1970s, Haitians continued to arrive in increasing numbers.

Following the riots, many blacks in Miami believed that the refugees exacerbated the situation. While we battled to secure financing to restore our broken towns, the Cubans soon established themselves as a major force in Miami. They received the majority of small business loans backed by the federal government.

While anticommunist Cubans were welcomed and granted refugee status, Haitian "boat people" and other Afro-Caribbean immigrants were detained at the Krome Detention Center and were ineligible for federal help intended for political refugees. That fueled further resentment. While there was undeniable friction between American blacks and Haitians, the Cubans' favourable treatment felt like another slap in the face to black people.

But my parents did not raise me to harbour hatred in my heart, and I was still too young to be tripping over any race nonsense. One of my best pals was a Chico named Raul. His mother was from Honduras, while his father was Cuban. We called him White Boy.

Between the drugs, the rioting, and the influx of immigrants, there was a lot going on. All eyes were on Miami. This was the era that influenced Scarface and Miami Vice. But, to me, everything felt natural. It served as my basis. I knew nothing else.

Despite the mayhem that surrounded us, 18301 Northwest 39th Court was a loving home. My mother was a busy person, what with her profession and studies—she'd returned to school to become a paediatric nurse practitioner. But she still found time to prepare a four-course meal for us every night. She prepared a variety of high-quality home-cooked meals, including pot roast, meatloaf, baked chicken, fried chicken, and liver, with cornbread and greens on the side and a dessert to finish. My mother makes an incredible strawberry shortcake.

My sister and I used to quarrel over the television in our den. Renee's favourite Hanna-Barbera shows as a child were The Smurfs, The Jetsons, and Scooby-Doo. As she grew older, she became interested in the era's black sitcoms, The Jeffersons and The Cosby Show.

I wanted to play video games. That was the most important thing for me back then. My father, a computer whiz, encouraged my hobby. He let me get all of the consoles. He had a Commodore 64 home computer, and I had an Atari 2600. Then I acquired the ColecoVision, followed by the Neo-Geo, and then the Nintendo and Super Nintendo.

Renee eventually obtained a TV in her bedroom, which ended the fights. My sister and I have always been quite close. Renee is a G. We are cut from the same cloth in many respects. All of the elder street niggas I became close to later in life. Niggas such as Kane, Black, Short Legs, Earl, Wayne, and even E-Class were buddies with my sister first.

Music was always present in our home and could be heard coming from my parents' old-school wooden stereo cabinet, which had an eight-track, record player, and radio. Because of the age difference between my parents, I was exposed to music from all generations and genres. My father played a lot of jazz. Miles Davis, Charlie Parker, Dizzy Gillespie, and all John Coltrane vinyl records. My mother was more into soul music and R&B. The Isley Brothers, Isaac Hayes, Bobby Womack, Curtis Mayfield, Tyrone Davis, and her fellow Clarksdale native, Sam Cooke. She adored gospel music, too. Mighty

Clouds of Joy. The Williams brothers. Mahalia Jackson. Rev. James Cleveland.

My introduction to hip-hop happened at school. I was in third grade when Luther "Uncle Luke" Campbell and 2 Live Crew released The 2 Live Crew Is What We Are, the first album that propelled Miami bass music from the city's underground clubs into the mainstream. Luke's harsh lyrics seemed to appear out of nowhere in the corridors of my Miami Gardens Elementary School.

"HEY-Y-Y-Y-Y WE WANT SOME PU-U-USSAY-Y-Y!"

Talking about a pussy was about the worst thing you could do as a third-grader. I was a class clown, so it wasn't long before I was singing it in the cafeteria.

These kinds of actions eventually got me kicked out of school. When I was in fourth grade, I had a young white man instructor. His name was John Gay. When he tried to encourage me to pay attention in class, I fucked with him.

"You cannot tell me what to do. "You are gay."

I assumed I could get away with stating that since it was true. The man's real name was John Gay. But the technicality did not save me, and my mother had to come in to deal with him. He explained that my poor grades were due to my classroom behaviour and a lack of seriousness about academics. He was probably correct, but my mother told him he didn't know how to connect with black boys, so she took me out of school that day and enrolled me in St. Monica Catholic School.

But when I kept bringing home Ds from private school, she took me back to Miami Gardens Elementary and persuaded my principal, Mr. Leon, to let me return. My mother was not about to spend $200 a month for me to receive the same grades.

"Well, I can't be here every other day," she said. "I have to work."

I ensured she wouldn't have to. From that point forward, I did enough to get by. I had given up on becoming a good student, but I cared about not being a burden. I knew my mother was telling the truth when she claimed she didn't have time for my nonsense. She worked as a nursing director at Landmark Health Center from Monday to

Friday, 9 to 5. On the weekends, she worked per diem at Miami General Hospital. On top of that, she worked ten hours per week as a nurse consultant.

For a while, my father also worked a lot. He taught accounting at Miami Dade Community College and was a co-owner of a real estate company with a subcontract with HUD. If a homeowner defaulted on their mortgage and the house went into foreclosure, his company would board up the house, trim the grass, and maintain the property.

But, as my father approached his eleventh year of teaching at Miami Dade Community College, he was laid off. After ten years of service in Florida, you become entitled to a pension. However, if they discover a reason to fire you before then, you would forfeit your pension benefits. They were making a lot of people dirty back then, and that's what happened to him.

My father could have done whatever he wanted in this world. The dude was very close to brilliance. I never asked him a question that he didn't know the answer to. But after they removed his pension, I believe he lost his motivation. He began spending more time drinking beers with his friends outside the corner store.

He still worked. He took a job teaching night classes at Florida International University and did people's income taxes on the side. But he wasn't a hustler like my mother was. Like my grandfather, she was always looking for the next opportunity, whether it was a promotion, another degree, or an extra shift at the hospital. As I grew older and became more conscious of these things, I learned that my mother was the earner in our household.

2 Live Crew had introduced me to hip-hop, but I didn't have somebody to direct my interest from there. My mother wasn't fond of profanity, and she was even less liked of the dirty shit Luke was referring to.

My interest in hip-hop only began to grow until Jabbar introduced me to Too Short. Jabbar was my best friend growing up. He still is. He lived three houses down, and he and I have been there since day one.

Unlike me, Jabbar had a slew of older brothers and cousins in the area who were constantly introducing him to new music. We were strolling over to the park one day when he handed me the headphones for his Sony Walkman.

"Fatboy, check this out," he said.

"Yo! "Who the fuck is that?" I asked.

"Too short," he informed me. "He's from Oakland."

This was the moment when hip-hop captured my whole attention. I needed to learn everything there was to know about it.

I began spending my lunch money on records at the Carol Mart, a flea market on 183rd Street and 27th Avenue. I still didn't know what I should be listening to, so I bought records based on the cover art. That's how "Walk This Way" by Run-DMC became my first piece of vinyl. I didn't even like the music, but the cover was chilling.

I'd bring my records home and go over every detail. When I bought The 2 Live Crew Is What We Are, I saw that the Jeep Cherokee they were riding in had "Luke Skywalker" written on it. I'd keep an eye out for that Jeep whenever I was riding about the city in the rear seat of my mother's automobile. I think it was amazing that they photographed the cover in the alley behind the Pac Jam. It blew my head to discover that the record had been pressed in the heart of Liberty City. I knew where those locations were.

Rebbie Jackson's 1984 track "Centipede" inspired me to write my first rap song. It was one of my mother's records, and the B-side contained the song's instrumentation. I'd listen to it for hours and jot down whatever rhymes I could think of. I wrote to that one beat for months, trying with different rhyme patterns and figuring out how to change my flow when the beat changed.

Miss Nelly, my music teacher at Miami Gardens Elementary, encouraged me to write raps with themes rather than just focused on having them rhyme. I followed her instructions, and my homie Bishop and I wrote a song called "Where the Hoes at?"

"Where the Hoes at?" was a song about the baddest girls from Miami's five major black high schools: Norland, Jackson, Northwestern, Central, and Carol City High. Each lyric referred to a different school and day of the week. I started the song with Monday and Tuesday, then Bishop and his older brother handled Wednesday through Friday.

Miss Nelly was not particularly fond of the subject matter of "Where the Hoes at?" but she appreciated that Bishop and I had taken our assignment seriously. She arranged for us to sing the song at a "Just Say No to Drugs" event in Carol City Park. That was the first time I had ever taken the stage.

Bishop and I were confident we had a hit record on our hands. We went on our bikes and cycled from Carol City to Miami Lakes. That is where Uncle Luke stayed. Luke had a big-ass house on the golf course, and we knew if we could get him to come out and sing this song for him, we'd be billionaires. There was no doubt in our minds.

We couldn't find Luke, and "Where the Hoes at?" was never the breakout hit Bishop had hoped for. But the praise and encouragement I received from Miss Nelly, as well as the reception from the crowd at Carol City Park, planted a seed in my mind. I was good at rapping.

Hip-hop would also introduce me to the world beyond Miami. I began finding artists such as Eric B and Rakim, Big Daddy Kane, N.W.A., and the Geto Boys. I'd never gone to New York, Los Angeles, or Houston, but as I closed my eyes and listened to the music, I was transported to the various worlds these people came from. I'd never met an Asian person in my life, but when Ice Cube rapped about racist Korean store owners bothering niggas in Los Angeles, I imagined myself standing outside the store, a forty-ounce in hand. My records become stamps on my passport.

Everything about the culture intrigued me. I decorated my bedroom walls with posters of LL Cool J, Big Daddy Kane, EPMD, Salt-N-Pepa, Special Ed, and MC Shan from Word Up! and Right On! magazines. I watched movies like Beat Street and Breakin' and learnt the four fundamentals of hip-hop: DJing, MCing, B-Boying, and graffiti. I was also obsessed with clothes. Eric B. and Rakim donned these Dapper Dan outfits on the cover of Paid in Full. Run-DMC wore Cazal shades. Slick Rick had an eye patch and had gold ropes around his neck. Cool C, a rapper from Philadelphia that I liked, wore a red silk sweatsuit and red suede low-top Bally sneakers with holes. Only the dope boys in Miami wear Ballys.

I recall being at the Carol Mart arcade one day and seeing the music video for Marley Marl and the Juice Crew's "The Symphony" on the big screen. There was a group of gals around, and the baddest of them began bragging about how great Big Daddy Kane was. Her mouth nearly watered. That day, I started to grow out my flat-top.

My lunch money and the few dollars I earned trimming neighbours' lawns and lugging old Spanish ladies' groceries to their cars weren't enough to keep up with the rate at which my record collection grew. So, when I was thirteen, I took a job at the car wash on the corner of 183rd Street and 27th Avenue.

On weekends, I'd be there between 8:00 a.m. and 8:00 p.m. A day's work cost $30 plus tips. I made sure I got some tips. When the dope lads pulled in, they got first-class treatment. I would wash their automobile, vacuum the interior, and degrease the seats if necessary. Before I finished, I would check their cassettes to see what they were listening to. Then I would arrange them alphabetically. It wasn't long before all the hustlers were asking "Windex William," the dirty little fat thug, to service their vehicles.

Hip-hop was no longer merely a hobby. It became a complete obsession. The way I gravitated to rapping was the closest thing I could imagine those junkies behind my house feeling when the crack smoke struck their lips.

Chapter 3

The 1980s saw the development of a new breed of kingpin in Miami. Cocaine was no longer solely for the elite, and crack had spread throughout the inner cities. It wasn't the Cocaine Cowboys vying for dominance of the cocaine industry anymore. It was the urban dope dudes. Ghetto stars and hood legends include Isaac "Big Ike" Hicks, Rick "The Mayor" Brownlee, Bo Diddley, Bunkie Brown, and Convertible Burt.

Jabbar's father was one of these hustlers. Big Mike. Mike was a true Geechi nigga from Liberty City. He had a curly perm and a mouthful of gold teeth. But behind his Cazal sunglasses were the eyes of a man who would not be fucked with. Mike was at a level where any number of young shooters would have gladly handled any issue for him, but he wanted to do his own dirty job. Mike went over to his sister's place when he discovered that the father of her son was still hitting her. Mike had advised this guy to stay away from his sister the last time he visited. This time he went home and fired two rounds into his dome. Then he nurtured his sister's boy as if he were his own.

Mike was a member of the original Miami Boys, a team that ran heroin and cocaine across the Southeast United States. We'll get into that more later, because Jabbar and I didn't get into much trouble during the first ten years of our acquaintance. We spent the majority of our time together playing with joysticks at the park or each other's houses. We would catch rides on the back of an ice cream truck and go fishing for bass and bream fish in the local canal. We needed to keep an eye out for venomous water moccasins. South Florida's seas are home to an incredible variety of species.

For a while, the baddest thing Jabbar and I did was fistfight. We battled a lot as children. With one another, as well as other children at school and in the neighbourhood. This was the age when you had to prove you had hands. Fighting was how you gained status and respect. The weakest shit you could be was a cur, a dog that did not fight.

Kello, one of the older boys who lived up the street from me, coordinated a large portion of the fighting. Kello was my official bully growing up. That's putting it nicely. Really, Kello was a psychotic monster. He enjoyed fighting and encouraging other children to do the same. He would organise his most high-profile battles for Friday and Saturday nights at the park, when everyone would be watching.

Jon-Jon and his cousin Steve served as Kello's criminal companions. Jon-Jon also resided on my street, and he was quite vicious. He considered wicked trash. I recall Jon-Jon coming to my place one morning and pounding on the door. I was still in my drawers when I walked out to see what he wanted.

"The Devil rode my back... The Devil ain't never rode your back, Fatboy?!"

"Nah...what does that feel like?"

"It's like you wake up but you can't move...your eyes are open but your eyes are closed..."

I am telling you. Something was very wrong with these niggas.

Steve was from Overtown, but he would ride the bus to Carol City to hang out with Kello and Jon-Jon. Steve had two gold front teeth etched with dollar signs, which he had obtained from robbing others. He planned to rob his way up to eight. It could be 100 degrees outside, and Steve would still be wearing his black sweatshirt and a black skully.

The odd thing is that Kello and Jon-Jon were both church lads! Kello attended church every Sunday with his mother. She was a huge black lady who resembled Florida Evans from Good Times.

One Sunday, Kello had to read Scripture in front of the entire church. When he started stumbling his words, I burst into laughter. Jabbar kicked me, knowing I'd live to regret it, but it made me laugh even harder.

Kello interrupted her reading in the middle of service to address me in front of the entire congregation.

"Boy oh boy... The things I'm gon' do to you..."

The next day, Kello invited me to come over. One thing about these boys is that if you didn't do what they said, whatever they had planned for you would just worsen. Kello was so frantic that if I didn't come over on my own, he would sit outside my bedroom window until I did. So I walked over there and brought Jabbar with me. Kello's mother was in the kitchen preparing hog maw and collard greens when he led me into his bedroom and closed the door behind us. That's when he gave me one of his mother's clothespins.

"Take your shirt off," he said. "Put this on your nipple."

"Excuse me?"

"Do not make me swing on you, boy. Simply put it on your nipple. "Sixty seconds.

For the first fifteen seconds, I kept it cool. I was in tears by the half-minute mark. By the end, I was certain I had split my nipple in half. Kello finally pulled it off and allowed me to go home.

But I liked Kello! All of his tormenting came from a place of love, which toughened both me and Jabbar. When it came to battling somebody our own age, we were so much ahead because we'd grown up fighting these older niggas who were skilled with their hands.

That was about the limit of my bullying growing up. Things took a turn for the better when Jabbar and I began riding our bikes to Miss Angel's place. That's when everything shifted from the ordinary boyish mischief of two jits arriving in Carol City to something more sinister. I was just twelve, yet I was rapidly exposed to a level of criminal activity that most adult men never witness.

Miss Angel was Jabbar's aunt, and she stayed in the Matchbox. The Matchbox, a beige two-story walk-up apartment complex near the corner of 199th Street and 37th Avenue, was renowned as the Carol City crackhead's home. It wasn't a particularly large project, but when it came to selling drugs, the place was on fire. That is why they named it the Matchbox.

Fat Sean ran the front section of the Matchbox. Sean was the wild, junkyard dog sort of nigga. He had a thick beard and a full mop of hair on his head that was never combed or brushed. However, the hair was in good condition. Sean resembles Chico. He'd be stationed outside his place, rolling dice or bickering with his bitch, with a couple of kilograms inside—hard and soft—ready to serve.

Canhead had control over the back of the Matchbox. Canhead was a small, light-skinned nigga with freckles and sandy red hair. I didn't engage with him much, but he was a cool nigga. He wasn't as brute as Sean was. Canhead was both a DJ and a hustler, and he would set up his turntables and speakers outdoors to host block parties for the Matchbox.

The majority of my time at the Matchbox was spent in the centre part. That's where Miss Angel stayed, and her apartment housed the headquarters of a group of men who would soon dominate Carol City. These guys were all many years older than Jabbar and me. This is where I met guys like Boobie, Graylin, Bernard, Fishgrease, Cat Eye Moses, and D-Green.

There was a lot of crap happening at Miss Angel's. A table crew may be set up in the dining area, slicing up the dope. They utilised cutting agents to stretch out the product, diminish its purity, and increase earnings. There may be a nigga in the kitchen mixing coke and baking soda in a Pyrex pot. I was at Angel's the first time I witnessed an ounce of powder being boiled down to a drop. The crack did not come out white like the coke. It had a yellowish colour. Wrapped in plastic, the zone resembled a macadamia nut cookie.

Kenneth "Boobie" Williams, one of the aforementioned hustlers, would go on to become the most infamous. When he came on America's Most Wanted a decade later, he was introduced to the public as the ringleader of the Boobie Boys, a ruthless street gang responsible for a $85 million drug ring, 35 murders, and over 100 shootings.

However, when Jabbar and I initially started hanging out in the Matchbox, there were no Boobie Boys. Boobie was not even present in the beginning. He was in Miami-Dade's Juvenile Detention Center, contesting a murder charge stemming from a shooting in River City in October 1987, which killed one and injured two.

If there was a leader on this team, it was Graylin. Graylin was only sixteen when I met him, but he had the body and presence of a mature man. He was the sort to battle ten niggas and come out on top. Graylin was a cold-blooded, violent motherfucker. His nickname was The Grinch.

Graylin was the first dope boy I recall seeing driving exotic automobiles. It was the late 1980s, and candy-painted donks were still popular in Miami. Box Chevys, Cadillac Broughams, and Fleetwoods are languishing in the 30s and lows. But sixteen-year-old Graylin showed up one day in a brand-new white BMW convertible. I remember him putting a dollar food stamp under the glass of his licence plate frame. So he wouldn't forget where he came from. I thought that was the coolest thing ever.

Graylin's Beamer was spectacular, but it was his proclivity for violence that left the strongest effect on me. There was one incident in particular. Graylin began flirting with a dancer named Pinky shortly after I started hanging out at the Matchbox. Everybody in Miami knows Pinky. She was regarded as one of Dade County's baddest bitches.

This put Graylin at odds with Pinky's jealous ex-boyfriend, one of Liberty City's most dreaded gangsters. He was a prominent player in the 22nd Avenue Gang. Now, I don't know all the facts of how this battle over a hoe began, but I do know how it concluded. Graylin approached this guy outside Jumbo's, a soul food restaurant in Liberty City, and blew his brains out. He simply rolled up to him in his drop top and fired fire. The end.

When the streets began to chatter about what had occurred, I couldn't believe it. I knew Graylin was ruthless. His notoriety preceded him. But the other guy was meant to be on a completely different level. He was in his thirties and had lived on the streets for decades, and this teenager had just knocked him down like nothing. It appeared impossible. The incident made a lasting impression on me. I realized then that any nigga could have it and any nigga could offer it. That none was exempted.

I wouldn't see Graylin for a long time after that. He fled for a few months until being apprehended in Tallahassee by federal agents. He received twelve years in prison for that, but he allegedly almost committed a triple murder while awaiting the outcome of the case. Graylin allegedly beat three other inmates to death with his own hands at the United States Penitentiary in Atlanta. He was acquitted of those accusations due to self-defence, but he would not be as fortunate when it came to the murder charges he faced back home. He pleaded guilty and received a 15-year sentence.

Graylin's best friend Boobie was returning home around the same time he went in. Boobie pled guilty to attempted second-degree murder in connection with the River City shooting and served a few years in juvie. When he returned home, he secretly assumed leadership of the Matchbox.

Graylin was a leader that people dreaded. He commanded respect by using force. Boobie was different. He did not drink, smoke, or use vulgar language. His leadership was based on finesse. He was a person that people genuinely liked and wanted to associate with. Now, don't get it twisted; Boobie was by far the most on-point nigga in Carol City history. He did not hesitate to drop the hammer when the situation demanded it, and he believed the situation demanded it frequently. However, it was not his initial inclination, as Graylin's was. There was a difference. He made more cerebral decisions. Everything was calculated. Unlike Graylin, Boobie had a method of concealing his iron fist by slipping it inside a velvet glove.

A youthful criminal mentality may see prison to be similar to college. Throughout his tenure, Boobie formed contacts with dope dudes from all throughout Dade County. Niggas in Liberty City, Overtown, Brownsville, Opa-locka, Little River, and Little Haiti. When he returned home, those contacts had expanded into a network of like-minded hustlers. That was how Boobie began to develop an empire.

Niggas like Fat Sean and Canhead had no ambitions beyond running their small businesses in Carol City, nor did they have the resources to do so. However, even as he rose to the position of kingpin, Boobie still carried himself with the dignity of an ambassador rather than a tyrant. His vision went beyond the Matchbox.

Miss Angel's flat was more than just a drug lab. It was an armoury where everyone stored their firearms. It was a safe house to hide in after a home invasion. Because, as much as Boobie and his crew were dope lads, they were also robbers. They were carrying out a major heist. If one of them was tipped off about a nearby stash house containing bricks, they would ski mask up and go get them.

They also targeted pawn shops and department stores. Miami is where smash-and-grab burglaries originated. They'd gather a few stolen vehicles and drive one right through the stores' front windows. They'd load up the others with as much jewellery, weapons, and clothing as they could and flee into the night.

Jabbar and I were sleeping at Miss Angel's the first time I saw them return from one of these excursions. They broke in in the middle of the night, arguing and fighting over who would get what. Whatever garments didn't fit them or small chains they didn't want, they gave me and Jabbar. We looked up to these niggas, who looked out for us. They may have tolerated us at first because they knew and respected Big Mike, but they gradually developed a true liking for us.

T-Man and Triece were the first niggas to confront me and Jabbar with crack. We were so young that we didn't know what to do with it. We simply knew we wanted in. So we brought it to Angel's son, Jabbar's cousin Arthur, who demonstrated how to cut it into various sizes of pebbles and described our profit margins.

We ultimately discovered that Arthur was robbing us. Because he actually lived at Miss Angel's, he knew where we kept our explosives, and when Jabbar and I went home for the night, he would cut up a handful of pebbles for himself from our stockpile. It was all love, though. Getting fined was one of the growing pains of understanding the drug game.

These guys understood we were too small to take over other niggas' corners, so they let us leave Miss Angel's. When a junkie came in searching for something small to keep him going until the next day, they'd send them our way so we could put a couple dollars in our pockets. They watched out for us.

When I look back at the route I started down, I can't say I didn't know better. My family was not wealthy, but we also did not live in roach-infested housing developments. Carol City was considered a middle-class community. It was a haven from the bloodshed that was raging in Liberty City and Overtown.

I grew up with two educated and successful parents. I could not blame them. Nobody was smoking crack. Nobody was beating each other. My father smoked too many cigarettes and drank too many

Michelob Ultras, but his vices weren't ripping our home apart. He was always quite smooth with it.

But, around the time I started hanging out at the Matchbox, my home life altered. My parents announced their separation to my sister and me when I was eleven years old. They had learned to love and respect one another over time, and they had provided a loving home for their children. But I'm not sure if my parents were ever in love in that sense. They did not have that kind of intimate relationship.

As far as divorces go, this one wasn't too bad. There was no bad mouthing each other or squabbling over money or the house. There were no attorneys involved. They handled things well. But my father moved back up to North Florida, and I didn't see him much after that.

My father's departure caused a void at home. My mommy had to work much more than she already did, and I began spending more time with guys like Boobie and Big Mike. The drug lads were my role models.

The feds claim Boobie and Mike were monsters who preyed on their own kind. But I saw a different aspect of the tale. Every Christmas, Boobie hosted a toy drive at the Omega Center, where hundreds of items were distributed to Carol City's youth.

So, to me, they were Robin Hood types. All of the "Just Say No to Drugs" messages I was receiving at school were warning me that drugs were wrecking a lot of people's lives. At the same time, I saw children's cheeks light up when they received their first bicycles for Christmas. The ethics of hustling were complex. The distinction between right and wrong was unclear.

When I initially started primary school, I hoped to be a good student. My parents were both quite intelligent, and I admired them very much. However, as the years passed, I realised that I was nearly retarded in school. Do you realise how badly I wanted to learn Spanish? The prettiest girl at my school was Puerto Rican, and she was my first love. She would come to class once a week wearing her favourite Menudo T-shirt. That was the boy band that all the Spanish females adored back then. I wish I could have said some fly Papi Chulo crap to her.

Maths was the worst. When it came time to study the multiplication tables, I experienced a mental block. My mother got me the flashcards. She once hired a tutor for me. I just couldn't remember those. That was the main reason I became the class clown. It was the only item in school that I received positive comments on.

But for some reason, when Arthur taught me and Jabbar how to break down an ounce, that was something I could understand. An ounce contains twenty-eight grams. A kilogram weighs 36 ounces. If I sell one gram for $50, it makes sense to me.

Big Mike attempted to keep us off the streets at first. He wasn't pleased that Jabbar and I were hanging out in the Matchbox. He knew what was going on at Angel's and did not want us to be a part of it. He'd sent Jabbar to Our Lady of Perpetual Help, the Catholic school in Opa-locka where all the dope boys' kids went, and eventually removed him from Miami entirely.

The trouble was that Mike never shielded us from seeing all of the money. Or his gold 500 SEL Mercedes with champagne leather seats and windshield wipers on the headlights. Or the bricks encased in cellophane. Or his.308 Winchester with a bubble level scope. You could shoot a nigga in another city with that firearm.

It's one thing to inform a couple of hits that selling narcotics is wrong. However, when you show them what a million dollars looks like and ask them to count it for you, the message is lost. Suddenly, Old Scrappy—as we called my father's Buick—didn't seem like a great enough car for me. Working at the car wash from 8:00 a.m. to 8:00 p.m. and sticking to the rules suddenly didn't seem so tempting. But Mike tried to warn us.

"Only one out of a thousand hustlers makes it," Mike would constantly say. "When you get older, you'll either be broke, dead, or serving a life sentence. Trust me, those are the only things that will happen.

It was too late, though. I'd already seen too much. I was obsessed with wealth. I became infected with greed.

Chapter 4

Football has always been popular in Florida, but it was a huge deal when I was younger. I was seven years old when the Miami Dolphins selected Dan Marino in the 1983 NFL Draft. Marino was first underappreciated. John Elway was unquestionably the crown jewel of that draft class. But that changed as soon as Marino received his first snap. He quickly rose to prominence as the franchise's spokesperson.

The 1983 football season also saw the University of Miami win its first national championship, defeating the top-ranked University of Nebraska Cornhuskers in the Orange Bowl. The Hurricanes would go on to win three more titles in 1987, 1989, and 1991, cementing their position as one of the greatest college football dynasties of all time.

It wasn't always this way. For years, the University's football program had been an embarrassment, and the administration was on the verge of discontinuing it. In a last-ditch effort to turn things around, the administration appointed Howard Schnellenberger as head coach in 1979. Schnellenberger served as Don Shula's offensive coordinator when the Dolphins went undefeated in 1972.

Schnellenberger shook the entire operation up. Even after he departed the U after that first victory, his impact on the school and the city endured.

We adored the Hurricanes teams because they were homegrown. Schnellenberger altered the entire strategy for scouting and recruiting high school talent. Instead of pursuing the same blue chips that every other coach was looking for, he focused on the hotbed of underappreciated talent in his own backyard. He began recruiting black lads from around South Florida to this wealthy white elite school in Coral Gables.

When 2 Live Crew arrived on the scene, they were fiercely patriotic. They donned Hurricanes Starter jackets on their record cover, and Luke was an unofficial supporter of the program. The U's accomplishment was something that black Miamians could be proud of and feel a connection to. Football helped the city heal after the race riots.

Statistically speaking, the chances of playing Division I football, let alone making the league, were minimal to none. But I was watching players like Melvin Bratton go from the streets of Liberty City to catching passes in the Super Bowl. I was watching Alonzo Highsmith get picked by the Houston Oilers. I was witnessing Richmond Webb, the Miami Dolphins' left tackle, driving around Carol City in his white-on-white Mercedes. Those stories made it seem attainable. It appeared within grasp. These people resembled me. They spoke like me. They were only somewhat older than me. Why can't it be me?

For starters, I was never allowed to play youth football. Pop Warner and the Optimist League had weight limits for their age divisions. I never exceeded such restrictions. For a thirteen-year-old, the limit was around 140 pounds. By the time I was thirteen, I weighed well over 200 pounds.

"Fatboy" was my nickname, yet it was never a source of embarrassment. I wore it like a badge of honour. I looked like my father, who had been a jock, a veteran, an educated businessman, and an all-around confident individual. I inherited his confidence. Even now, the Roberts men carry their weight effectively. I wouldn't say we're overweight. We're just some beefy, attractive niggas who smell nice.

I was too fat to play football with my pals, which was not a pleasant sensation. I wanted a trophy. There was a coach who let me practise with his squad during the week, but on game day, I had to watch from the bleachers alongside the other spectators. That was slightly embarrassing. I once bought a sauna suit at The Sports Authority in an attempt to lose weight. I quickly understood it was not going to happen. I was not even close.

When I got to high school, my weight no longer kept me from playing football. Instead, it became an asset. Alfonzo Morgan was in the same boat with me. I don't recall how big Fonzo was when we met for tryouts our freshman year, but by senior year, I was six-foot-two, 292 pounds, and he was around six-foot-five, 330 pounds. We were huge lads.

Coaching the Carol City Chiefs required a unique set of skills. Our team was comprised of a group of wild niggas. We used to break into our rival schools at night, smashing trophy cases and spraying fire extinguishers everywhere. We would vandalise the entire area.

Walt "Big Money" Frazier, one of the best high school football coaches in Florida history, was the only one who could keep us under control. The nickname was a joke. We nicknamed Coach Frazier "Big Money" because he wore the same clothes and train conductor hat every day. We never saw him spend money. We assumed Frazier must have a lot of paper stashed somewhere.

Frazier not only taught us how to play football, but he also taught us much more. He was a father figure to youngsters like me and Fonzo, whose fathers had both moved away and died. He taught us how to be men and ingrained in us the importance of hard work and discipline.

Frazier ran practice like a drill sergeant, and he did the same thing with us off the field. One time, Fonzo and I were acting up in English class, and our teacher asked him to intercede. He approached us during practice that afternoon.

"I told Ms. Maniscalco to send you two jackasses to my office the next time y'all want to act up," he informed them. "When you get there, I'll turn over my desk. Then I'm going to break the legs off the table and hand them to you...so you can protect yourself against me."

Frazier wasn't lying. The man was fearless. A shootout broke out in the crowd during a game versus our rivals, Miami Northwestern. When Nigas began shooting, everyone fell to the ground. Everybody, except Frazier. He didn't even move.

"Coach, get down!" one of us cried. "We need you!"

"I bleed orange and black!" Frazier screamed back.

I wore number 61 in honour of the roadway that my grandfather used to travel from Clarksdale to Memphis for work. After learning the fundamentals, I began to dominate my opponents. The Chiefs' offensive line was ferocious, and we hit so many pancake blocks that we became known as the IHOP Boys across our conference.

I got quite good. The Miami Herald named me to the All-Dade first team offence during my senior year. A lot of people thought I had a promising career as a football player. Coach Frazier. My teammates. My peers. My parents and sister. I believed in myself, too. But I never received recognition from the person I believe I desired it from the most. My father. Our relationship had been at a stalemate since he moved away, and it hurt that he never showed up for one of my games. I wanted Big Brewster to witness what his son was doing on the football field.

As much as I enjoyed playing football, I lacked the tunnel vision and complete concentration to the game required to excel at the highest level. By the time I went to high school, I was already involved in various extracurricular activities.

I'd graduated from selling nickels and dimes in the Matchbox and was beginning to gain some weight. One of my first experiences with this occurred when I was hanging out at Jabbar's place one afternoon and noticed Big Mike dumping many garbage bags full of cannabis. Mike was getting a lot of pot from the Bahamas and Jamaica back then. He had his own speedboat and would drive down there to pick up loads personally.

This particular batch had turned nasty. Mike's house's air conditioning had failed, causing roughly two hundred pounds of damage.

"You're really about to throw all that away?" I was wondering.

"It ain't no good," he replied.

"We could put carrots in it," I said. "I heard carrots preserve weed."

Mike knew where I was headed and didn't want to hear anything. He quickly focused his attention on Jabbar.

"Boy, don't you dare go trying to sell this garbage with this dumb nigga," he was saying. "He's going to leave the house with a thousand dollars' worth of this bullshit and come back with $995 worth, five dollars in cash, and a lump on his forehead."

I was not going to be discouraged. Mike did not consider a loss like this to be the end of the world. It was the expense of doing business.

However, that seemed like a lot of money to throw away. So I climbed in and took everything out.

It took a while, but Jabbar and I eventually sold every ounce of that nasty cannabis. We named it "Headbanga Boogie" since smoking it would give you a headache. The carrots surely did not solve the situation.

More weight equals more money. And more money equaled more issues. By ninth year, Jabbar had dropped out of high school and was living on the streets. I was still in school and playing football, but at least one foot was securely planted. The situation was intensifying.

Jabbar lived in a rooming house in Liberty City and had built up a shop there. Eventually, the niggas who claimed the neighborhood were aware that someone was short-stopping their block. These niggas hustled outside the business up the street, and Jabbar was grabbing their customers before they arrived, offering better dope at higher pricing. They showed up at Jabbar's location and informed him he needed to find another place to sling.

Jabbar did locate a different location. He stopped selling from the rooming house and moved to the park. But he must still be impacting these guys' pockets since they turned up and stated he couldn't hustle there either.

"We'll see where I can and cannot hustle, then," Jabbar told them.

At that point, Jabbar contacted and told me about the situation. I got him up and drove over to the business where these niggas hustled. I made Jabbar wait in the car while I shouted at the crew commander, who had commanded Jabbar to step down. I informed him that he was my brother, and that any problems he had with him would also affect me. Things became tense, but we left before anything more than words were exchanged.

I may have stated something about us claiming Carol City because a few hours later Boobie knocked on the door of Jabbar's rooming home.

"What's up with you niggas?"

"Nothing... What happened?"

"You gon' sit here and tell me you two ain't got no problems with these niggas around here?"

"Well, yeah, me and Fatboy—"

"I already know," Boobie replied. "Because these niggas were talking about running up in this house and killing y'all."

"So what are we fitting to do?"

"Nothing. They heard you were from Carol City, so their big homies contacted me, and I told him to grant you a pass. But you niggas are insane. Jabbar, you have a short stop where you lay your head. And, Fatboy, you're out here driving your mother's car and pulling up to niggas. "Both of you should fucking relax."

This wasn't Boobie's first time defending us. On another occasion, Jabbar and I drove past and sprayed up the block of the individual who had disrespected us. Nobody was hit because we weren't aiming at anyone. We were only attempting to convey a message not to fuck with us. However, the message got a little lost in translation.

The nigga we rolled up on also had difficulties with Boobie, for other reasons. But they assumed our drive-by was on Boobie's behalf. When Boobie discovered that these niggas were launching an attack because two young guys in a gray Cadillac opened fire on them, he came to visit us.

"Look, I ain't gonna be taking on all this beef for you niggas if y'all ain't even getting out the car and killing," he said with us. "You get out, you walk up on your target, and you shoot, you understand?"

My first arrest occurred when I was sixteen years old. I had once again taken my momma's Baby Lac for a drive. Fonzo and I were on our way to a house party when we stopped at an Opa-locka trap to pick up a bag of cannabis. As soon as we started hand-to-hand, the crackers pulled us over. It was a sting.

The Baby Lac was impounded, and Fonzo and I were transported to the Opa-locka police station, where we were detained on drug and handgun charges. I had a.22 in the car when they pulled us over. After we were photographed and fingerprinted, they were ready to transport us to Miami-Dade County Jail beside the real wolves. We attempted to tell them we were only sixteen, but Fonzo and I were so huge that they didn't believe us. Luckily, my mother arrived at the station before anything happened and got us out. She found a lawyer who was able to seal the case. That was the first time my mother realised I was getting into trouble. Even so, I managed to play it off quite well. Fonzo had taken the gun charge, and I had taken the drug possession charge, so she still thought I was doing nothing more than smoking some marijuana.

I still received recruitment letters from a few Division I and II schools that were interested in having me play football. Florida State University. Colorado State. Clemson. But everyone thought I was going to the University of Miami. At school, I received another moniker, "Big East," because it felt like a given that I'd be joining the NCAA's Big East Conference.

My mother felt otherwise. She was not enthusiastic about me staying in Miami. Aside from my arrest, I had done an excellent job of keeping her in the dark about what I was up to. But she realised I didn't have to be a dope boy to get killed, nor did I have to be a killer to get an 187. She was concerned that I would become involved in anything unrelated to me. That I'd be riding in one of my friends' automobiles when something popped off. Depending on how things transpired, I could either catch a stray gunshot or be charged with complicity to murder.

My mother was also uncomfortable with me attending what she deemed a "white school." Our family has a history of attending black colleges. She knew Wayne Campbell, the assistant football coach at Albany State University, an HBCU in Georgia. Wayne was able to persuade the school to award me a full scholarship, and he pitched me on the notion of joining Albany State's Golden Rams football team.

The Rams had won their conference the previous season, and several former players had moved on to the NFL. Wayne told me. Instead of sitting on the bench at one of the larger D-I institutions, I'd be able to make a significant contribution at Albany State. To be honest, I'm not sure if Wayne convinced me or if I just wanted to please my mother. In any case, I've opted to attend Albany State.

When I arrived for preseason in the summer of 1994, the school was in poor shape. Tropical Storm Alberto had devastated the Southeast United States a few weeks prior, killing 32 people and causing more than $1 billion in property damage. The downpour was so heavy that the Flint River spilled, drowning Albany. The newspapers described it as Georgia's biggest natural calamity ever.

It was not a great start to my collegiate career. Because two-thirds of Albany State's campus was submerged, we were forced to live in trailers at a neighbouring military post rather than dorms. Without a proper field to play on, the team spent the first several weeks of preseason assisting the Red Cross in their relief work. I didn't mind, but the living condition was an issue. I wasn't doing a lot of drugs at the time, but I did keep a pistol in my room and was heavily smoking pot. So I had a lot of trash that I had no right bringing onto a military base. It was a recipe for catching a case.

As a crab—that's what they call freshman players—I didn't have many opportunities once the season began. But I liked what Albany State was accomplishing with its football program. I liked Wayne and the rest of the coaching group. I liked my teammates. Fonzo transferred to Albany State from a junior college in California, and the prospect of rejoining with the IHOP Boys piqued his interest.

If playing ball was all I had to do, I might have stayed. However, I was unable to complete all of my schoolwork. I was failing my classes and had no desire to put forth the effort to pass them. My schooling was the last thing on my mind. I was living the life of a broke college student, and all I could think about was how much money I was missing out on by being there.

When I travelled out to my grandmother's house in Mississippi for Christmas break, I told her I didn't think college was for me.

"But, Will, your mom is a nurse practitioner. Your father is a professor. "You should go to college."

She knew my mommy would be crushed. My sister had recently enrolled at Mississippi Valley State University, where she had previously studied. My uncle Tudor went to Tuskegee University, while my aunt Carrie went to Rutgers. All of my cousins, on both sides of my family, had attended college. My mother was responsible for securing me a full-ride to Albany State, and now I wanted to quit school after my first semester.

I did return after the winter break, but I was counting the days until the end of the school year. I didn't know what my future held, but I was certain it wasn't here. I ended the school year and moved back home.

Chapter 5

When I returned to Miami, I went back to Pac Jam. The Pac Jam Teen Disco, located on 84th Street and Northeast 2nd Avenue in Liberty City, was Uncle Luke's underage nightclub. Whether you were thirteen or thirty, from Liberty City, Carol City, Overtown, or Opa-locka, the Pac Jam was the place to go on Friday and Saturday nights.

Monday through Friday, the two-story facility operated as Luke Records' headquarters. But once the weekend arrived, the first-floor warehouse would be cleaned out and transformed into the Pac Jam. The walls would be lined with speakers and subwoofers stacked on top of one another. Then the Ghetto Style DJs, local luminaries such as DJ Amazing Chico, would arrive to spin booty-shaking bass music for over a thousand Miami youngsters.

Throughout high school, I was a "Pac Jam Junkie," a moniker that could only be earned if you attended every Saturday. My friends and I would get fresh beforehand. You could see me in Pac Jam wearing a new Tommy Hilfiger polo and a pair of trousers that had just come back from the dry cleaners. To achieve the desired crease, we applied strong starch to our jeans. I wore the gold Saint Lazarus pendant around my neck, a Figaro bracelet on one hand, and a Guess watch on the other. I didn't have any money yet, but I had a blueprint for how to get it.

Around the time I moved back to Miami, Luke organised a talent event at the Pac Jam, with the main prize being a deal with Luke Records. Pursuing my music seriously had been on my mind since I graduated, but I wasn't prepared to perform at the Pac Jam. It wasn't the most welcoming venue for performers. This is where Scarface and MC Lyte were booed off the stage. Its renown had earned it the moniker "Apollo South."

That night, a thug from Liberty City's Pork-N-Beans projects took the stage and stole the show. His name was Maurice Young, often known as Trick Daddy Dollars. Trick had recently returned home from a two-and-a-half-year stint in state prison. It was inspiring to witness him take down the Pac Jam and land a record deal. It made me think. Maybe I can actually do this.

I ran across one of my former elementary school instructors not long after. Miss Anderson. She was saddened to learn that I had dropped out of college, and when she inquired as to my plans, I informed her that I had quit school to become a rapper.

"You know, Will, my son has been making beats," she told me. "I think you two should meet."

Miss Anderson's son was named Rod. As a producer, he went by Sharp Shoulders. For a high school student, he made some decent beats. He had been studying how to use a mixing board at Reel Sounds, a new recording studio in Miami Lakes. It was owned by Earl, his cousin. He invited me to come check it out.

Earl was making a lot of money, and I knew it from the moment we met. Earl was pouring with diamonds. He had multiple necklaces, a diamond pinky ring, and a platinum Rolex iced out with big-ass stones all over the band and bezel. This was before everyone started busting down Rollies. Earl's '75 Chevy Caprice convertible was parked outside the studio, sitting on chrome Daytons. Baby blue with white intestines and a white rag-top. Earl owned various automobiles.

Earl remembered me. He graduated from Carol City High in 1991 and was friends with my sister's then-boyfriend, a guy named Griff. Griff had been a dope guy until the day he was slain in Virginia, so Earl's affiliation with him was all I needed to know Earl was making money on the streets.

Reel Sounds was Earl's legitimate business enterprise. He spent six figures on this cutting-edge studio. It included hardwood floors, state-of-the-art recording equipment, plus an upstairs lounge and office. The property was quite beautiful. After hearing a few of my raps, Earl invited me to work out of his studio at any time.

Along with launching the studio, Earl founded M.I.A. Productions, an independent record label. In his earliest attempts to find talent, he came across a half Jamaican, half Puerto Rican youngster with matted dreadlocks freestyling in Carol City Park's pavilion. His name was Richard Morales Jr., also known as Gunplay.

Gunplay could rap his ass off, but he was a loose cannon. Gun was only sixteen, but he had dropped out of school, been arrested, and was slinging and snorting powder. He was unsure of his next step. Was he going to be a drug dealer, a robber, or a rapper? I admired Gunplay and took him under my wing. We soon found ourselves together every day, both at the studio and on the street.

I'd been creating raps since elementary school, but Earl's studio was where I really got my start as a songwriter. Prior to that, I would create fifty-bar verses, link three of them together without a chorus, and call it a song. Now that I'm working in a real recording studio with other emcees, producers, and engineers, I'm shortening up all of my verses to sixteen bars. I became aware of how I wanted my voice to sound on wax and began layering vocals and performing ad-libs. I asked my old friend Bishop, who had worked with me on "Where the Hoes at?" to record choruses. Bishop had grown up singing in church and was able to harmonise well.

Gunplay, Bishop, and I formed a group named Triple C's, also known as the Carol City Cartel. I was Willow, the group's sole lyricist. Bishop carried the ghetto gospel. Gunplay was a wild card. He was Miami's version of "Old Dirty Bastard." You never knew what you would receive from him.

The first version of Triple C's did not endure long. I quickly knew we'd have to locate a successor for Bishop. Bishop had a lot of talent but couldn't stay out of trouble. He was constantly in and out of jail, making it impossible for us to build any momentum as a group.

I was in the studio one day when a girl called and said she had a younger sibling who could spit. His name was Torch. Earl had been putting up signs throughout the neighbourhood to promote Reel Sounds and seek for talent. When she got Torch on the phone and he started rapping, I was astounded. Big sister wasn't lying. Torch's punchlines were savage, and his delivery was devastating. Gunplay didn't believe Torch had actually written his bars, so we invited him to the studio to see if he was serious.

Torch was not from Miami, as I could tell from our phone talk. Niggas from the crib tend to speak and rap slowly, while Torch had the language and delivery of a New York nigga. When he got to the studio, he told us his entire story. Torch came from the Castle Hill housing community in the Bronx. He'd gotten caught up in some street shit, so his mother had sent him to live with his sister in Fort Lauderdale. He'd been keeping a low profile there, but like the rest of us, he was hoping to make it big in the rap game.

From that day forward, Triple C's consisted of Gunplay, Torch, and me. We began locking in at the studio every night. We had Sharp Shoulders and a couple other producers—shoutout to Ree Dog and Troy Bell—cooking up beats, and Earl would be in there flaunting all the money he was making. Earl used to pull pranks on us. Like Earl, I had a blue Chevy Caprice, but mine was a raggedy four-door with wheels that looked like they were about to fall off at any moment. My grandfather had given me that automobile. I recall Earl once clowning Gunplay for his attire while some hoes were hanging around at the studio. Both of them wore football jerseys that day, although Gunplay's was a screen-printed copy and Earl's was the actual one with stitched-on numbers and inscriptions. Earl also joked about it. He was putting salt in the game! But hey, I love and appreciate my big homie Earl. All of that was trivial crap. Earl opened the doors to his studios and offered me and Triple C's an opportunity when he didn't have to, with no monetary gain for him.

Eventually, we got a compilation of tunes we were pleased with. We created a mixtape and had several hundred copies produced at Kinko's. We initially attempted to sell them, but this proved unsuccessful. Miami lacked an established mixtape market, unlike Houston, where you could almost go platinum selling cassettes from the trunk of your vehicle.

We changed our tactic and began giving away the recordings for free at every flea market, strip club, and after-hours location from West Palm Beach on down. We'd give DJs a few dollars to play our songs, hoping that one of them would catch on in the clubs. But that didn't produce fantastic outcomes either. The problem wasn't only that Miami residents didn't buy mixtapes. The actual issue was that Miami didn't really promote up-and-coming artists unless they had Luke's endorsement.

The aim was to keep grinding in the hopes of catching the notice of an A&R or executive from a large label. If we could strike a deal, the city would rally behind us. It didn't matter if we got a collective deal for Triple C's or a solitary deal. Earl never placed any of us under contract. There was basically an implicit agreement that if one of us took off, they would return and bring everyone else with them. The difficulty was that none of us planned to take flight anytime soon.

The music was moving slowly. The streets, however, told a different story. Things were accelerating for me. Fast.

To go to the next level of hustle, you had to leave town. It was difficult to lose weight in Miami since cocaine was so cheap and plentiful. Everybody had access to it, and the competition was fierce. This was particularly true for the Carol City niggas. Carol City was not like Liberty City or Overtown, where you could sell marijuana all day in front of massive projects. With the exception of the Matchbox and the flats behind my house, Carol City was primarily made up of single-family homes. There was only so much money to make here.

Big Mike had departed Miami a long time before. The crib had been ground zero for the Miami Boys, but after law enforcement became aware, they moved north, taking over every city in the Sunshine State and setting up traps throughout the Southeast United States. Georgia, Alabama, Tennessee, Louisiana, Kentucky, and the Carolinas extend all the way to Virginia. It was a basic introduction to colonialism.

Mike had tried to keep Jabbar and me off the streets, but when he noticed it wasn't working, he took the opposite strategy. If we were going to do this anyway, we'd rather do it under his supervision and away from the violence in Miami. Mike had provided Jabbar with an apartment in Atlanta as well as a kilo, and he had let his boy handle the rest. Jabbar did not require much guidance. If you give a Delancy any drugs, they'll know what to do with them.

Mike had eluded arrest by not becoming greedy. He would work in one spot for six months and then take a six-month break. Then he'd start again somewhere else. His method not only kept him one step ahead of the law, but it also allowed him to build a large clientele throughout the Southeast.

Mike began sending me on jobs that required the conveyance of either drugs or money. There were only a few gun runs. The directions were simple. Get an automobile. Not the same as previously. Pick up. Deliver. It wasn't brain surgery, but it kept me busy. I began making regular travels up and down Interstate 95, from Miami to the Carolinas.

Mike and Jabbar stood out from the other hustlers I encountered because they were in the boy business. The majority of my heroin dealings occurred in Jacksonville, where the demand was as high as in Miami but just a few people had access to it. I began bringing stuff up to Jacksonville from Miami. I'd generally spend a few days up there while niggas worked off the pack to get me money to bring home. But I didn't enjoy being around that garbage. I never used heroin, but I felt like I might have become addicted just by being in the same room and inhaling that filth while it was chopped up with chemicals like quinine and mannitol. If I spent a few days with the boy and then went home, my stomach would start to hurt. This happened to me several times. I was basically going through a mild detox.

Then there were the testers. Whenever I sold heroin, the customer would bring a tester to determine the vibe. I will never forget this one, nigga. He claimed to have six pairs of eyes, and if he went on boy, he would see all this crazy stuff and tell us about it. To be honest, the nigga was hilarious, but the entire thing was so messed up. I'm not sure why, but everything about dealing with heroin disturbed me more than it did with crack. The dealers. The junkies. The sense of selling something for days on end. The only thing I really enjoyed about it was the money. The money from the boy arrives faster.

What began as a courier job soon evolved into me spreading out and developing my own customer base. I began networking in the many cities to which I was bringing jobs. I'd go to strip clubs and meet girls who knew a local dope boy looking for a Miami plug. The next time I went to these areas, I wasn't just driving. I had my own clientele there.

I gained a foothold in the Florida Heartland, where I had cousins on my father's side. I drove up there once to bring one of them some work and realised Central Florida was ripe for the picking. I soon began taking trips up the Florida Turnpike to Bartow, Belle Glade,

Melbourne, and Okeechobee. These were undeveloped markets where I could control the price. I could run these country places!

Even after I set out on my own and began creating my own plays, I realised I was a part of something far larger than myself.

When it comes to music, I can proudly declare that I am self-made. However, when it comes to the drug trade, I must acknowledge that I benefited from nepotism. From the beginning, I had friends in high places. Everything was laid out for me. I was part of something. A system that was in existence long before I arrived. I just continued adding to it.

Chapter 6

The year 1998 was a significant turning point. The feds began cracking down on everybody. Hard.

Things had been heading that way for a time. Ronald Reagan's War on Drugs messed up the streets. The Sentencing Reform Act of 1984 abolished parole and created mandatory minimums, requiring offenders to serve at least 85% of their sentences. Two years later, at the height of the crack epidemic, Congress passed the Anti-Drug Abuse Act, which required a five-year minimum penalty for possession of five grams of crack. However, if you were caught with the powder, you would have to have more than 500 grams to receive the same punishment.

A minor modification to the Anti-Drug Abuse Act in 1988 landed a lot of my homies in jail. The conspiracy amendment makes it possible for everyone involved in a conspiracy to be held liable for any crimes committed during that conspiracy. The lookout child or explosives man were now receiving the same penalties as the kingpin. Due to court case processing delays, the full impact of these laws did not become apparent until the 1990s. That's when niggas began snitching.

But it wasn't just the weight the niggas were carrying that eventually killed them. They were also dropping bodies.

On September 6, 1992, Boobie was shot five times in the parking lot outside Club Rolexx, a notorious Miami strip bar. They claimed Boobie attempted to give it to a nigga, but his gun jammed, so the guy gave it to him instead. Boobie had scars all over his stomach and needed to wear a colostomy bag after that.

The shootout at Rollexx began an era of crime, similar to the Dadeland Mall incident in 1979. The Miami Herald named it "A Decade of Death." When these opposing gangs waged war on one another—the Boobie Boys in Carol City, the Thomas Family in River City, the John Does in Liberty City, and the Vondas in Overtown—Dade County became a battleground. They began going tit for tat after the killings. On any given day, at any given time, cars full of niggas wielding sticks drove around the city looking for an enemy to shoot at.

In 1996 and 1997, Miami was the United States' murder capital. The headlines triggered the creation of a federal task team to put an end to the violence. Their inquiry gave rise to the whole "Boobie Boys" phenomenon. That was a moniker coined by the government to allow them to pursue all of their targets under the umbrella of organised crime rather than having to investigate all of these unsolved shootings individually. Boobie was a mentor of mine, and we performed plays together, but I was never a lieutenant under him or a member of any gang. It didn't work that way.

On February 23, 1998, the task force announced the results of their investigation, attributing thirty-five deaths and more than a hundred shootings to gang warfare between the Boobie Boys, the Vondas, the Thomas Family, and the John Does. When the federal indictment was issued a month later, Boobie did something I had never seen him do. He ran.

Four months later, the feds raided Jabbar's hideout in Southside Jacksonville. I almost missed that raid. I had been in Jacksonville the week before. The indictment named Big Mike, Jabbar, his cousin Tarvoris, and a few others in a decades-long conspiracy to distribute cocaine and heroin throughout the Southeast United States. The feds claimed Jabbar had followed in his father's footsteps and taken over the family business.

I discovered what happened at 30. 30 was my and Jabbar's little friend. He attended Miami Central with J and ran with us in Jacksonville. He was riding shotgun in Jabbar's Chevy when everything went down. One of Mike's previous collaborators had tipped them off that the feds were on their way. He had caught up with them and removed his top to reveal that he was wearing a wire. But we've never trusted this guy. J assumed he was trying to get them to leave the trap so he could steal the cache or money they had hidden in the back. Jabbar's strategy was to go over there, receive the money, and then leave town for a short time to be safe. But when they arrived at the residence, there were agents everywhere. 30, being the wild nigga he is, was ready to drive them at high speeds, but Jabbar urged him to stop. There was nowhere to flee. They had them.

The feds hauled 30 in for questioning, but he was not included in the indictment. They confiscated the five bands he was wearing, but later released him. But first, they asked him about me. Throughout their surveillance, the agents had spotted 30 and Jabbar arrive and depart in a truck with a large black fat nigga. It was my automobile. A two-tone candy-painted Dodge Ram 1500 with seventeen-inch chrome Daytons.

With everything going on, it was too hot for me to stay in Florida. I had to get out of Dodge. 30 was in need of a place to lay low, just like I was, and he mentioned he had an older sister in Marietta, Georgia, where we could stay. We picked up Kase, one of our 30s mates, and headed out.

When we arrived at the residence, we were greeted by Tomcat, 30's brother-in-law. Tomcat had no idea we were on the run when he opened his door to us, and he certainly had no idea we'd be sleeping on his floor for the next three months.

30 persuaded Tomcat to let us stay with him by introducing him to two of his rapper friends. Tomcat was working as a runner for an ambulance chaser lawyer at the time, but he was also a self-taught audio engineer looking to carve out a niche for himself in Atlanta's rap scene. He wanted to put Kase and myself together in a group called The Connect.

I wasn't very keen on joining another organisation. I already had triple Cs. However, Kase had a bit of a buzz back home. He had been included on Trick Daddy's most recent album. This made him far more established than I was. Aligning myself with Kase may not be a bad idea.

One of Tomcat's lawyers claimed to have a line on Shaquille O'Neal. This was back when Shaq was in the rap game and had his own Universal Records brand, T.W.Is.M. (The World Is Mine). I assumed this lawyer was faking it, but he truly came through and arranged for us to see Shaq at the All-Star Cafe on Peachtree Street.

Kase and I took turns freestyling for Shaq for more than an hour. Shaq's excitement grew with each quip I dropped. One line in particular grabbed his eye.

Shaq got up from his seat and took a lap around the restaurant after that.

We left that dinner meeting confident that The Connect would be offered a deal at T.W.Is.M. But a week later, the lawyer Tomcat had been in contact with was indicted on money laundering charges. Tomcat was unable to contact Shaq's manager again, which effectively ended the situation. The Connect failed soon after, and Kase returned to Miami.

The T.W.Is.M. situation had failed, but Tomcat quickly introduced me to two key figures in my early music career: DJ Greg Street and Russell "Big Block" Spencer.

Greg Street is best known as the host of The Greg Street Show on Atlanta's urban radio station, V-103. He is extremely prominent in Southern hip-hop and has had a role in many success stories from south of the Mason-Dixon Line.

The same might be said for Block. Niggas are familiar with Block as the founder of Block Entertainment, which is home to Boyz N Da Hood and Young Joc, but this goes back much further. I originally met Block while I was seeking a cannabis connection in Atlanta.

Block had good cannabis, but he also had many connections. Block used to hang out with Tupac and the Outlawz when he lived in Atlanta, and he introduced me to Pac's cousin Kastro. Then he took me to Noontime Studios, where I met and began to develop contacts with industry players such as Henry "Noonie" Lee, Ryan Glover, and Chris Hicks. Block connected me with a lot of folks in Atlanta.

Tony Draper was the most important person that Block and Greg Street introduced me to at the time. Tony Draper founded Suave House, the Houston-based label that launched the careers of musicians such as 8-Ball and MJG, Crime Boss, Tela, and South Circle. Draper had collaborated with Block and Greg Street to help him develop a Suave House presence in Atlanta. He could see the city was brimming with talent and ready to explode. Draper was establishing a Suave House satellite office in Dunwoody, but in the interim, he had put up a recording studio in Greg Street's basement at his Stone Mountain home.

Greg Street had Tristan "T-Mix" Jones stay with him. T-Mix was Suave House's in-house producer, and he created the signature Memphis sound on all of the early 8-Ball and MJG albums I grew up listening to. That sleek, flying, player pimp crap.

Greg invited me to work out of his studio, and as soon as he did, I knew I'd be there every day until someone told me to stop going. I was a huge fan of 8-Ball and MJG, so the opportunity to record with T-Mix was something I couldn't pass up. It would be my first time working with someone who knew more about music than I did.

Greg Street's friendliness extended beyond the complimentary studio time. I would raid his fridge for meals, and when Tomcat wanted a break from entertaining me, Greg would let me stay the night.

Block was handling an artist named Lil Noah and had convinced Tony Draper to sign him to Suave House. Noah had skill, but he was inexperienced when it came to composition, so I began assisting him in putting together albums. Draper eventually learned that there was a big nigga in Greg Street's basement writing all of Noah's rap songs. So he flew to Atlanta to find out what the Teflon Don cat was all about. That was the moniker I was known by at the time. I'd repainted my Ram pickup purple with phantom flames and had "Teflon Don... Album Coming Soon" painted on the sides.

I was astonished to see how young Draper was. He was only a year older than me and had already done so much in the game. It is one thing to do this as an artist. Rapping is mostly a sport for young men. But as an executive and CEO? To emerge from the dirt and do everything on one's own? That thing was impressive.

I was working with Noah on a song called "Bird Bath" when Draper turned up at the studio. He only needed to hear my verse. As soon as I got out of the studio, he informed me that he wanted to sign me to Suave House.

"What's your name?"

"Teflon Don," I informed him.

"You're my next 8-Ball, Tef," he announced. "You're the next Biggie."

After I signed with Suave House, Draper began dragging me from city to city, taking me to various music conventions and introducing me to his industry contacts. He had an impressive list of contacts.

Draper brought me to Houston's Fifth Ward, where I met and played basketball with J. Prince in the middle of the night. J. Prince founded Rap-A-Lot Records, and in my opinion, he was just as pioneering as Luke. J. Prince inspired a sixteen-year-old Tony Draper to begin Suave House, and he cleared the path for niggas like Master P to launch No Limit Records and Bryan "Birdman" Williams and his brother to start Cash Money Records. Rap-A-Lot served as the pattern for establishing an independent hip-hop label in the South.

Draper understood that meeting a Southern royalty like J. Prince was a dream come true for me, but he wanted me to rhyme over some East Coast rhythms. So he flew me to New York to work with Redman and Erick Sermon. Redman picked me up from the airport in his BMW X5 truck. I could not believe he had come to collect me. Red was high on the success of Doc's Da Name 2000 and Blackout!, both highly praised and platinum-selling albums.

Before heading to Erick Sermon's crib on Long Island, we stopped in Harlem to pick up a jar from Branson. Branson was the iconic cannabis man to the celebs. I'd heard his name mentioned in Redman, Biggie, Ma$e, and Rakim's rap songs. He was the idea for "Samson," the drug dealer character in the new stoner comedy Half Baked, which stars Dave Chappelle.

I hadn't even been in New York for an hour, yet everything felt unreal. I was truly here, sitting in the back of Redman's truck. We had just picked up pot from Branson and were now on our way to Erick Sermon's residence. Redman was a bona legitimate celebrity at the moment, but it was the fact that I was about to record a few records in The Green Eyed Bandit's basement that really got me. I grew up during rap's golden era, and EPMD had a significant influence on me. I'm getting ahead of myself, but my entire "Maybach Music" series of songs was inspired by EPMD's "Jane" saga, in which every album they released had a new song that continued the "Jane" character's story.

As we rode past Shea Stadium, I recall pausing to take in the moment.

This ain't no ordinary crap, homie. This means something. Make it count.

One of the songs we recorded that week, "Ain't SHHH to Discuss," ended up on Erick Sermon's 2000 album Erick Onasis. This would be my first appearance on a major label album. E-Double still has an unreleased record from back then that, if heard now, would fuck people up. I'd be remiss not to mention that. We'll get that Michael Jackson sample cleared sometime, big friend.

After one of these trips, Draper informed me he had a surprise for me. When I arrived home, there was a gift. I opened it and nearly shed a tear. He had sent me a Rolex watch. It was my first time, and it was not a disaster. It wasn't a regular Jane either. It was frosted out and included genuine Rolex diamonds. That bitch was mint.

I've always been a watch enthusiast. I consider myself a collector of clocks. When I was younger, all I could afford was Geneva and Guess. Those were the days when I daydreamed about the Breitling Emergency watch, which would summon a helicopter if you pulled the pin. Once I had money, I began accumulating it. I received the Audemars Piguet that Arnold Schwarzenegger wore in Terminator 3. Dr. Dre once gave me a $100,000 Hublot as a birthday present, while Drake gave me a Presidential Rolex.

However, none of those watches have the same sentimental importance as the Rolex Tony Draper gave me in 2000. The watch was not an advance. It was not his manner of repaying me for whatever. There were no strings tied to it. It was simply a gift given from the goodness of his heart. A method for him to express his appreciation for me as an artist and friend.

Draper had no idea how much this present meant to me. That's because I never told him how broke I was. After Jabbar's indictment, I decided to take a break from the streets and focus on my music. That decision had harmed my finances. I spent what little money I had on maintaining my appearance. I kept my appearance fresh, and I always had a pleasant trip. At some time, I returned my demonstration truck for the new Cadillac Escalade. But my life was far from as glamorous as I made it out to be.

When I went to Houston to visit Draper, I had to sleep in my car since I couldn't afford a hotel. Draper would show me around and introduce me to all of the game's legends, and I seemed to fit right in. Scarface approached us in his black 600 Benz outside the Sharpstown Mall on Houston's southwest side—right at the corner of Fondren and Bellaire Boulevard—and I didn't feel out of place. I resembled an established artist. But at night, I'd find a rest spot on the highway and pull over to sleep for a few hours. When I awoke, I'd meet up with Draper as if I'd just left the fucking St. Regis.

Draper would never have let that happen if he knew I needed a place to stay. But I didn't want him to know it. I did not want to appear like a beggar with my hand out. Even when I first met Draper and was sleeping in Greg Street's basement, I gave the appearance that I was a big boss, a wealthy guy. I also had him misled.

Chapter 7

A few months had gone since the feds apprehended Jabbar, so I believed it was safe to resume making a few plays back home. I needed money. The issue was that none of my main partners were available. Jabbar was arrested, and Big Mike and Boobie fled. That string of events wreaked havoc on Miami's drug trade ecology.

Mike changed his look and fled the nation. He'd transitioned from a curly perm to a high top fade and removed his golds. He was hiding out in the Bahamas with his cousin, Samuel "Ninety" Knowles. Samuel was a much greater kingpin than Mike, with cribs all across the Caribbean. When the indictment was issued, Mike departed the United States and began island-hopping from one location to another.

Boobie stayed in town, and we kept in touch long after he left. I'd occasionally go up to Atlanta to see him, or he'd pop into Miami for a quick visit. I couldn't recognize Boobie then. He'd changed his complete appearance. I was used to seeing Boobie dressed in his New Era suit down to his white Air Force Ones, but suddenly he looked like a nerd. Boobie used to drive the Ford Mustang 5.0 GT convertible that Kane drove in Menace II Society, but every time I saw him, he was in a new vehicle. Never anything that would draw notice. Always something inconspicuous.

With my days gone, I began running with a new group. Earl was collecting money with a staff from the Venetian Gardens housing developments. This set of guys—Kane, Black Bo, Short Legs, Skinny—got along with a lot of the niggas I knew from the Matchbox because they all represented 37th Avenue. They also came up under Big Mike. We quickly became close friends and accomplices in crime.

This is also around the time when I began dealing with Wayne Parker. Wayne was Boobie's associate, and he had a big-ass crib in northwest Dade County, where my sister and her friends would hang out. I'd known Wayne for a while, but we didn't start conducting business until Troy invited me and Jabbar over to his place one day.

Troy was Wayne's protégé. I, Jabbar, and Troy all had four-wheeler ATVs at the time—maybe in '97 or early '98. We'd raise hell on our banshees. We'd ride through the city, doing donuts, wheelies, and weaving in and out of traffic. When the cops arrived, we would drive them away at high speeds. Getting the city police to come after us wasn't bad. We'd take it a step farther and get on the roadway to draw the Florida roadway Patrol's attention. That meant the radio call was broadcast across the state!

On one particular chase, we were zooming down the turnpike and exited at Joe Robbie Stadium. We took a couple of side streets and when we realised we'd lost them, Troy pulled us over to Wayne's house. Wayne had a massive ass crib with exquisite Roman porch columns in front. His lawn was beautiful, and behind the gates stood a full fleet. There were many Mercedes. The S500 has two doors and a large four-door body. I knew they cost $150,000 each. Then he had a black cherry Chevy Tahoe sitting on dubs. A blue-on-blue 1975 Chevy drop-top. Fully stocked BMWs and Acuras. There must have been ten whips out there. To this day, the way I line up my cars outside my house is modelled on how I saw WP living in the 1990s.

Wayne went out of the house wearing a silk robe. He held a glass of champagne in one hand and a joint of some sort in the other. Wayne always had the greatest cannabis. Before meeting him, I'd only smoked Reggie and Jamaican yard marijuana. Wayne was the first to introduce me to the high-power crap. On his wrist was a $100,000 platinum Rolex. The only niggas I'd ever seen wearing that watch were Puff Daddy and Sisqo. WP was a flashy playboy.

"How y'all youngsters doing?"

"We just shook the crackers!"

"Well, enjoy yourselves and stay safe. Please let me know if you need anything from me."

I did not start doing business with Wayne until Troy was imprisoned in 1998. Boobie and Mike were both on the run, so I took Troy's place as Wayne's understudy, and Wayne took on the mentor role that I had with individuals like Mike and Boobie.

But Wayne was not like Mike or Boobie. Wayne wasn't a gangster. He was never involved in any of the violence that these two were constantly engaging in. Wayne's DNA did not include any of the crap that leads to body drops, such as robberies and hitting licks and juugs. His success was due to his skill as a salesman and chemist. There were very few niggas who could cook crack as well as Wayne did. All of his junk was picture-perfect, and he never walked on anything. He simply sold a lot of dope calmly and reaped the benefits of his labour.

Even though Wayne was not a gangster, he was so well-respected that no one would ever try him. I remember one night we were at Club Amnesia and got into it with some niggas. We were about to bring out our pistols when Wayne walked in and told everyone to calm down. He didn't raise his voice or say anything. He was really calm. And everyone acknowledged him. There were few niggas with the ability to do so, and those who did were usually vicious. WP was ahead of his time.

I figured the feds would never catch Big Mike. He was the last of the Miami Boys on the run. His two collaborators, Causey "Silk" Bryant and Ike Florence, had been incarcerated for years. Silk was sentenced to life in prison in 1989, while Ike received a twenty-eight-year term in 1993.

I didn't think the feds would catch Boobie, either. He moved with extreme caution. In all of my years knowing Boobie, I can't say he ever handed me a package. Not one time. I'd always come across things somewhere else. In the trunk of my car or in a garbage can outside my residence.

Mike and Boobie were very similar. Two Virgos who paid special attention to the slightest things and planned their manoeuvres meticulously.

But by the spring of 1999, everyone's luck had run out. Mike made a short mistake in judgement, which was the slipup the feds had been waiting for. He returned to Miami after suspecting that his spouse was cheating on him. He returned not just to the United States, but also to his home. That was a really unusual mistake for him. They put Mike on some bad crap.

They kidnapped Boobie in Clarkston, Georgia, a month later. Boobie did not make the same mistakes as Mike. The amount of attention he received became overwhelming. There was a $56,000 reward for information leading to his arrest, and the Miami Herald covered his manhunt every other week. After appearing on episodes of Crimestoppers and America's Most Wanted, it was only a matter of time. He was held in a tight grasp and unable to move. There was too much heat on him.

Two weeks after the feds apprehended Boobie, I met Wayne Parker at Miami Lakes Studio Center. I was dividing my time between Atlanta and Miami, and I was looking for a new recording location when I was at the crib. I wasn't recording at Earl's studio anymore.

However, this was before home studios, therefore it would cost $155 per hour plus an additional $55 for an engineer. That was for Studio Center's bare-bones C-Room. That's why I tried to convince Wayne to pay for my studio time. Wayne recognized my skill and was willing to invest in my career. However, he had some constructive comments for me. He said I was rapping too quickly and should slow down my bars so people could comprehend what I was saying.

It was raining when Wayne and I exited the studio. It was June 1, 1999, the Tuesday following Memorial Day weekend. The hurricane season had begun again. We smoked a joint, then Wayne dropped me off at my mother's place. The plan was to meet up again later that night with a couple of our friends at a comedy concert in Coconut Grove. However, when I arrived at The Improv, Wayne was not present.

"Fatboy, you heard about Wayne?"

My heart skips a beat. In Miami, when someone begins a sentence with "You heard about...", it usually signifies someone has died.

"What happened?"

"You were just with him, right?"

"Yeah."

"When he returned to his crib, the Marshals were waiting for him." They say he was indicted in Pensacola. I've never known Wayne to go up there, but you know how it goes. Niggas has been telling, and the feds aren't playing fair."

After the feds extradited Mike to the Jacksonville pretrial detention centre, I drove there to see him and Jabbar. They were held in separate sections, so I started by seeing Jabbar. As soon as I sat down, he placed a stack of paperwork against the glass that separated us. That was his indictment.

Jabbar's indictment included over fifty unindicted co-conspirators. His mother was listed. His younger sibling. His ex-wife. Rick "The Mayor" Brownlee, a well-known Miami drug boy, was among those listed. Then I saw my name. It simply said, "Will, aka Fatboy."

Jabbar moved to the following page, which proved that the feds had been keeping an eye on us for a time. As I read the story, I remembered we had seen these guys observing us one night at The Silver Fox, a strip club on Jacksonville's westside. At the time, we assumed they were jackals plotting to rob us. We stepped up to them and pulled our pistols. It never occurred to us that they could be undercover spies.

"Look, they don't know who you are and I didn't fill in the blank for them," Jabbar responded to my query. "But they know the truck."

"I'm not driving the truck any more. So, what's the game?"

"Ain't no play."

There were numerous flaws in this indictment, which was entirely based on testimony from secret informants. Jabbar and I were born the same year, 1976. But, according to his documentation, he had been conducting a vast multi state heroin operation since 1983. He would've been seven years old at the time.

"Your lawyer must be all over these mistakes, right?" I asked him.

"You really don't understand how this shit works until they come, Fatboy," Jabbar thundered. "And then it's too late."

When I went to visit Mike, he informed me that I needed to sit for a bit. He wasn't interested in seeing me take up the torch.

"Get a job somewhere." "I am not asking you; I am telling you," he said. "Remember when I used to claim that just one out of every thousand hustlers succeed? "Go become a fireman or something."

I was pretty rattled up when I left the prison that day. Football had not worked out. College had not worked out. Now everyone was being indicted. Jabbar has previously accepted a plea agreement. He was going to spend a dime in federal jail.

Six months later, Mike was convicted of the same counts. They gave him 30 years. A few weeks later, they gave Wayne thirty-five. The way things were going for Boobie, he'd never get out. Boobie's case was very different. He was dealing with bodies.

It seemed like my entire universe was collapsing on me. My two closest friends and mentors, Troy and Jabbar, and now Mike and Boobie, had departed from my life. And then my father died.

In September, the physicians informed him that they had discovered a spot on his lung. Within months, the cancer had advanced to his liver. He had tumours the size of golf balls all over his body.

As a computer nerd, I'm sure my father would have liked to see how the Y2K stuff played out. But he did not. He died in December. He was 64 years old.

Even though my father and I had been estranged for years, I knew that our love was still there. He had gone to Mississippi to be closer to Renee, and I knew one day I'd drive out there, chop it up, and get back solid. It screwed me up that I was incorrect about it.

Why did my father die so young? Was it all those years spent in phosphate mines? Was it the cigarette? Or was there something else? I'd never know. The unspoken words between us would remain unsaid. Because I did not have the heart to be the one to start our reunion. Even today, I wish I had.

Block drove to Clarksdale with me for the funeral. I was in a lot of pain, but it felt numb. More than the sadness, I recall feeling lost. I was looking for guidance. However, there was no one left to turn to. Everyone was gone. As I put my father's casket into his grave, the same thought kept playing through my head.

What the fuck should I do?

Chapter 8

It became evident that my situation at Suave House was not improving. Draper was coming to Atlanta less and less, and he eventually stopped answering the phone. I was recording a lot of songs but had no plans to release an album. I was not the only one. Draper had signed a slew of artists to Suave House about the same time he signed me, including Noah, Gillie da Kid, Coo Coo Cal, Psychodrama, and the Ill Hillbillies, and none of us had any upcoming releases.

The writing was on the wall when I realised Block and Greg Street had moved on to new projects. Block had given up on Noah and taken over as head of A&R at Noontime Records. Greg Street was also working on a Southern rap compilation CD for Atlantic Records titled Six O'Clock, Vol. 1. I was meant to be on that project. Greg Street paid me $5,000 for a song I wrote called "Willy Bananas" in what was my first feature payment. Greg didn't retain me on the album because Atlantic preferred bigger names, but he did let me keep the five stacks.

Tony Draper's second chapter of Suave House had not gone so smoothly. In 1998, Draper helped finalise Cash Money Records' $30 million distribution deal with Universal Records. Draper wants to emulate Cash Money and No Limit Records by signing artists and releasing albums on a regular basis. However, Universal was not interested in doing this with Suave House. They were only getting behind the 8-Ball and MJG releases.

So, in 1999, Draper ended his distribution arrangement with Universal and formed a joint venture with Artemis Records, releasing the 2000 Suave House compilation CD Off Da Chain, Vol. 1. When the record failed, Draper backed out of the arrangement and formed a partnership with another company, JCOR Entertainment. That arrangement turned out considerably worse for him.

While Draper was involved in a litigation with JCOR, his painters began leaving Suave House. On top of that, Draper may have been involved in some street crap. I knew he wasn't attempting to keep me on the shelf, but I also knew I wasn't high on the priority list.

When a label's CEO gets into trouble, the performers usually follow suit. But Draper did not want it to happen to me. He wanted me to win, whether it was at Suave House or elsewhere. So, before I could become upset and consider my choices, Draper approached me with an offer to sign with Slip-N-Slide Records.

Slip-N-Slide was not merely the most popular label in South Florida. It was one of the most popular labels in the rap game, period. Slip-N-Slide, founded in 1994 by Ted "Touche" Lucas, became a local household name with the publication of Trick Daddy Dollars' 1997 first album, Based on a True Story.

I first saw Trick Daddy at the Pac Jam in 1995, when he won the talent show and signed with Luke. However, the agreement never came together. Luke was forced to declare bankruptcy and let go of his whole team. But what Luke considered a squandered chance turned out to be a blessing in disguise for Trick. He was doing quite well at Slip-N-Slide. His second album, www.thug.com, sold over 500,000 copies, and the hit tune "Nann Nigga" exposed the world to a second Slip-N-Slide star. A wicked bitch from Liberty City named Trina.

Trick's success, combined with Trina's ascension, raised Slip-N-Slide's prominence to a national level, resulting in a major-label joint venture with Atlantic Records. Even though Slip-N-Slide was the best, I had a lot of reservations about moving over there.

For starters, I wasn't particularly interested in joining with a Miami-based label. When it comes to my music, I didn't feel like I received much love at the crib. I'd spent a lot of blood, sweat, and tears trying to get my career started in Miami, and I hadn't seen much of a return on my investment.

The Luke era's up-tempo booty-shaking music served as the foundation for Miami hip-hop. With the rise of JT Money and Poison Clan, followed by Trick and Trina, the city's sound began to develop. But it was still not what I was doing. Trick was the live, breathing embodiment of the Pork-N-Beans projects from which he sprung in Liberty City. He was rapping for thugs with dreadlocks and permanent gold teeth. The niggas that spiked their blunts with cocaine. We call it boonk.

I was a large gorgeous nigga who aspired to be wealthy. I wanted a half-million-dollar automobile, a three-million-dollar house, and a lovely hoe in a bikini next to me in the jacuzzi. You need to understand. Niggas in Miami weren't rapping about boss shit like that back then.

I was putting on for the city, but my ambition extended beyond Miami. Trick was the voice of niggas who would never leave the projects. I couldn't limit myself to that. I couldn't simply rap about donks. I was looking at the new Maybachs that Mercedes-Benz had just unveiled. I couldn't simply rap about wearing Dickies. I had ideas of myself at the Met Gala wearing silk Versace textiles. I couldn't simply rap about eating conch, mangos, and Jamaican meat patties. I wanted Del Frisco's marbleized tomahawk steaks.

There were so many things that were still out of my reach. I couldn't buy cars or clothes yet. Places I had never been before. People I'd never met. These were the things that filled my mind and kept me up at night. Of course, they became part of my music. I was rapping both my reality and my destiny. I was speaking things into existence.

The other reason for fear about contracting with Slip-N-Slide was some old street trash. There was the possibility of complications with Trick Daddy's camp. I didn't know T-Double personally, but I was a fan of his music, and there had been previous incidents involving Boobie and Trick's people that may result in lingering bad blood between us. When Trick's brother Hollywood was murdered in 1994, rumours circulated that Boobie was involved. Boobie constantly disputed this, but as the word spread, many people in the city accepted it as fact.

Hollywood had not only been Trick's brother. He was also best buddies with Ted Lucas. They had planned to create a record label together. Plus, Hollywood was dating Trina at the time of his death. Slip-N-Slide was a close-knit group formed in response to a family member's death. I was hesitant to sign there in case I was perceived as an enemy due to my relationship with Boobie.

But Draper told me that Ted wanted to sign me, so perhaps that wasn't the case. While he and Ted negotiated a business agreement, my big buddy Kane took the initiative to explore if we could make this alliance work on a personal level. Kane knew Josh, Ted's partner at Slip-N-Slide, and arranged for us to meet at the Carol City flea market.

Josh was from North Glade, a Carol City neighbourhood just west of where I'd come from. We'd never met, but we had a lot of mutual acquaintances and associates. My first impression of Josh was that he was friendly but reticent. But Kane had told me Josh was very, very, very certified in the streets. Josh came from a long history of hustlers and was Versace Neal's disciple. Versace Neal may have been the wealthiest nigga on the streets at the moment. Neal was someone you only heard about. You would never see him pull up to any of the popular hangouts for dope boys. He had too much cash for that. So Josh was a Triple OG just by association. Over time, I realised Josh's soft-spoken manner was a red herring. Josh was similar to Mike Tyson in that judging him just on his kind demeanour would give you no notion of his true abilities.

Josh and I chopped it up, and a few days later he brought me to Trick's studio. Trick played me a few tracks from his upcoming album, and we even discussed working on some music together. Once I realised there was no pressure from him, I began to consider signing with Slip-N-Slide. After Ted struck a deal with Draper to buy me out of my Suave House contract, I did exactly that.

The day after I signed with Slip-N-Slide, Josh took me to Studio Center in Hialeah, where I met Duece Poppi, an Atlanta rapper who was supposed to be the label's next big thing. Deuce eventually changed his name to Whole Slab, thus whenever I mention Deuce, I mean Slab, and vice versa.

Deuce and I had a difficult start. I wanted to make it apparent that I would be the label's next talent to debut. However, when I discovered that Deuce knew Boobie, I changed my stance.

After fleeing to Atlanta, Boobie began hanging out with Duece's major friend, a guy named Dixie Fare. Dixie was another Miami nigga who had relocated to Atlanta, and his name rang bells in the crib. So I lightened up on Deuce, and we quickly became friends. But I was still determined to make an impact at Slip-N-Slide from the start. Deuce and I recorded a song that day, and I spewed a verse that drew everyone in the studio's attention.

Talking about fucking Trina on day one of Slip-N-Slide raised a few eyebrows. I ended up modifying the sentence to "Have you ever seen Trina?" but I still got my point across. I was the label's new whiz. I was here to shake up the entire operation.

Josh handled Trina, and they were starting to work on her second album, Diamond Princess. He had heard about my pen game and saw me as a valuable asset to the studio. After my work with Noah failed to produce results, I wasn't interested in doing any more ghostwriting, but if this was my way of paying my dues and proving my worth, so be it.

I soon found myself going around with Josh every day to various studios throughout the city. Audio Vision and Circle House are both located in North Miami. Rare Breed Studios in Carol City. Poe Boy Studios is located in Little Haiti. House of Fire, South Beach. What began with me composing for Trina quickly evolved into collaborations with every artist on Slip-N-Slide's roster.

My first big glance was, "Told y'all." "Told Y'all" was a song I created for Trina in Cool & Dre's studio. Cool and Dre may be in London today, producing for Jay-Z and Beyoncé, but they were once an unknown team working out of a makeshift studio in Cool's mother's house.

Initially, I recorded "Told Y'all" as a reference track. Something Trina could utilise if she opted to forward with the recording. But when Ted heard the song and thought I sounded great on it, he instructed me to compose another verse for myself.

It was already a big deal to get a spot on Trina's record, and it only got bigger from there. "Told Y'all" was picked as the main song for the soundtrack to the big motion picture All About the Benjamins, which stars Ice Cube and Mike Epps. I had a small cameo in one of Noah's videos, but "Told Y'all" was my first big-budget music video.

I was at Studio Center one day when I met Kanye West, a twenty-five-year-old Chicago-based producer. Kanye was collaborating with another artist down the hall. We both had our own sessions going on, but during our breaks, we started conversing and he played me some of his tracks. This was Kanye's chipmunk soul era, and I enjoyed how he chopped up samples.

Kanye ended up working out of Studio Center for the entire week, and we continued our practice of having these tiny cyphers throughout our breaks. He'd play his beats as I spewed raps over them. By the end of the week, Kanye had told me he wanted to executive produce the entire record. I wasn't ready to commit to everything just yet, but I did want to get some of his beats. Kanye's tracks were cheap back then.

I ended up with two of them. One was for me—a real soulful joint that sampled a song called "I'm Just Doin' My Job"—and the other for Trina. That became her big single with Ludacris, titled "B R Right."

I met Kanye a few months later at the Diplomat Resort in Hollywood on the set of the "B R Right" music video. We were both waiting around the set, trying to get cameos, and we did. Kanye can be seen getting off Ludacris' tour bus at the beginning, and I get out of a taxi cab at the conclusion. If you blink, you'll miss any of us.

It wasn't quite the moment in the spotlight we were expecting. Kanye had received a lot of accolades for his work on Jay-Z's album The Blueprint, but his goals extended beyond becoming the in-house producer at Roc-A-Fella Records. Kanye wanted to rap, but his label didn't take him seriously. Meanwhile, I was making plays at Slip-N-Slide, but not my own. I was still throwing other people alley-oops. "Told Y'all" was a terrific look for me, but there had been no follow-up to build on it.

Before we left, Kanye and I agreed to get back in the studio shortly. But the week before we were set to meet, I learned Kanye had been in a terrible automobile accident. He fell asleep at the wheel following a late-night studio session in California, resulting in a head-on collision. He'd had reconstructive surgery on his shattered jaw, which was now wired shut, and he'd be bedridden for the foreseeable future. It would take eight years before Kanye and I met paths again.

In August 2002, Slip-N-Slide had two huge releases: Trina's Diamond Princess and Trick Daddy's Thug Holiday. Both debuted in the top 20 on the Billboard 200 and were later certified Gold by the Recording Industry Association of America.

Slip-N-Slide's reign was still running strong, and I was delighted to have contributed to its success. I'd written the two biggest songs from Trina's album and received three Trick placements. I had established myself to be a valuable acquisition. Now it was time to bring in the next big thing from Miami. Rick Ross. I was ready to come out of the shadows. It was the only reasonable next step.

That's not how things turned out. As part of Slip-N-Slide's joint venture with Atlantic Records, Atlantic had first refusal on signing its artists. Atlantic had provided me with a limited recording budget to make an album, and I had spent the previous year working on it alongside other Slip-N-Slide projects.

But when Ted showed my album to Craig Kallman and Mike Caren, Atlantic's president and vice president of A&R, they didn't like it. They put us back to the drawing board, stating I needed a more commercial song.

For a little moment, we were pleased with one of them. Saint Denson produced it and sampled Freda Payne's 1977 song "I Get High (On Your Memory)." Unfortunately, I was not the only one who heard the beat. It eventually got to Styles P of The LOX, and his people at Interscope were able to get the song despite Styles being the far more established musician at the time. That song proved to be a major success for Styles.

After that song fell through, we attempted another single called "Just Chillin," which featured Trick, Kase, and Gunplay. It did not shift the needle. Mike Caren then informed Ted that Atlantic was not interested in putting any more money behind me. They were all focused on Rick Ross. Without their support, I was warned that I would have to throw my record away. Just like that, the rug was torn out from beneath me. I was pretty much back at square one.

I then learnt that Craig and Mike had returned to Miami and signed Pretty Ricky. I was passed over for an R&B boy band. That news devastated me.

Underneath my jealousy, I was actually delighted for Pretty Ricky. Those boys had been doing their thing since the late 1990s, and they had also paid their dues. We would occasionally use the same circuit. HBCU homecomings and TJ's DJ music conferences. I always enjoyed seeing their synchronised acts and witnessing the hoes lose their wits. The stage would be covered in glitter following their performances. On top of that, Blue, the boys' father and manager, was well-known in the crib. I would never be anything but supportive of their accomplishment. They deserved it.

But in my thoughts, terror had begun to set in. Was I ever going to get a break?

Those crackers preferred Pretty Ricky over me... Oh, God... Oh my God.

Chapter 9

I was still signed with Slip-N-Slide, but we weren't on good terms. I felt like as soon as the situation with Atlantic deteriorated, Ted returned to concentrate on his two breadwinners, Trick and Trina. That did not go over well with me.

This is when E-Class became my manager. E-Class is the creator of Poe Boy Entertainment, a local independent label. I'd known E-Class since middle school, but he wasn't into music back then. When I met E-Class, he was dealing crack and cutting hair. He was friends with Renee, and anytime he got a break from trapping in the flats behind my house, he would stop by and hang out. Before my junior prom, I had E buzz a Louis Vuitton logo into my hairline.

E got heavy on the streets before launching Poe Boy. In 1993, he was indicted on conspiracy charges in Tallahassee. However, unlike most of the niggas I knew who caught cases around that time, E-Class outperformed his. He saw his acquittal as a sign to pursue a more legitimate career.

The name "Poe Boy" honours a fallen soldier, Kenin "Poe" Bailey, a close buddy of E-Class's. I also knew Poe. He led a very chaotic street life. He and E-Class had planned to venture into the music industry jointly, but they needed seed money. So Poe devised a plan to set up a check-cashing store in Miramar around the time people were receiving their tax refund cheques. Poe had an inside guy in the building—a barber who worked next door. Poe snuck into the barbershop's ventilation system via a ceiling panel and spent the entire night above the check-cashing area. When the employee arrived at work the next morning, Poe dropped down like Tom Cruise in Mission: Impossible and instructed him to put all the money in the bag.

But the dude fought back, and the entire lick shifted left. When the cops arrived, Poe fled the site. He attempted to hijack one of the cruisers. He was shot several times before he managed to peel free. The hunt did not last long. Poe was bleeding profusely. He crashed the car, and it was all over. They evacuated him out, but he died before the helicopter arrived at Jackson Memorial Hospital.

E-Class enlisted the support of his younger brothers, Chuck and Freezy, to get Poe Boy off the ground. Chuck was the number guy. He had worked as a mortgage broker for Barnett Bank in Miami Lakes. After marrying one of Flo Rida's seven sisters, Freezy discovered and managed another successful Carol City performer, Flo Rida.

E-Class didn't have enough money to buy me out of my Slip-N-Slide contract and sign me with Poe Boy. All of his resources were invested in a female singer he was promoting dubbed Jackie-O. So he became my manager instead. He and Alex "Gucci Pucci" Bethune, Poe Boy's vice president, took on the responsibility of managing me on a daily basis.

Josh was still the big homie, but at the time, E-Class was a better fit as my manager. E-Class was a Haitian silverback gorilla. He was willing to take a more proactive approach to promoting my career. That was a good fit for us. That's how I was feeling then. The manner I moved throughout the city. Aggression was my calling card. All of the disappointments had taken their toll on me, and my tolerance had worn thin. I had a short fuse, and niggas were getting slapped left and right for whatever I saw as disrespect. So I didn't need someone to respectfully ask DJs to play my songs. I needed somebody to tell them to. Someone who would enter a bar or radio station and not leave until my record was played. E-Class was the guy.

For a nigga like E-Class, the rap game was more of a way to make money without going to jail. Pucci was more of a music enthusiast. He was less rough around the edges and knew how to network in the sector outside of Miami. E-Class and Pucci each had strong suits, and as a team, they functioned well.

In an interview with Larry Dog, a well-known Miami comedian, I was asked to give some advice to aspiring artists. I glanced directly at the camera and stated, "Never sign a Ted Lucas contract." That video is still available on YouTube. Deuce was standing beside me, and you could see he felt the same way I did. Ted had not invested any money in the release of Godzilla Pimpin. No music videos. No promotion. Nothing. Deuce wasn't as outspoken as I was when it came to expressing his dissatisfaction. I let my nuts hang.

Trick and I never had an issue with the street shit, but tension did build between us. I believe Trick saw me as a danger to his position as the top dog at Slip-N-Slide. To be fair, Trick wasn't doing the most outrageous things. It didn't take much for me to get from 0 to 100. Trick didn't pay me straight away for opening for him one night, so I confronted him backstage and began bragging about being the true "Mayor of Miami." Trick did not want any complications.

Slip-N-Slide wasn't the only target in my sights. I began criticising T.I. for referring to himself as the "King of the South." I was claiming that it belonged to me, but I was really resentful that he ended up with the beat for "Doing My Job," the song I had originally written with Kanye for my album. It was a song off T.I.'s Trap Muzik album, which had just been released by my buddies at Atlantic Records.

If a radio DJ didn't play my tunes, they were played loudly. Just ask Big Lip Bandit and Supa Cindy, the hosts of The Big Lip Morning Show on 99 Jamz. I sent out a diss, stating all sorts of nasty things about them. I truly had a crush on Supa Cindy. I assumed she was fine as heck. She was a war casualty.

Even DJ Khaled and I had a tense meeting. People recognize Khaled as one of my long standing friends and allies in the music industry, but I saw him as yet another gatekeeper holding me back.

The Arab attacks. The Dondada. Big Dog Pitbull. Beat Novacane. Khaled was more than just another radio DJ spinning music in the 305. He was the DJ, and his endorsement reached far beyond South Florida. Khaled was breaking national records. The enthusiasm he put into releasing a song made it feel like something revolutionary was happening.

Khaled had gained a reputation as a tastemaker, and his success story appeared unlikely. Khaled was born in New Orleans to Palestinian immigrants. He travelled to Orlando as a youth before settling in Miami in the early 1990s. Khaled had dabbled with the streets a little bit—I believe he used to sell counterfeit cell phones and served time in county jail for driving with a suspended licence—but his true passion was always music.

Khaled had been DJing high school events in Orlando, but it wasn't until he moved to Miami that he began to establish his presence on the airways. He began his career spinning Caribbean tunes on Miami's pirate radio station Mixx 96. After catching Uncle Luke's attention at a party, he got a position as co-host of The Luke Show on 99 Jamz. When he received his own evening show, his career really took off.

I didn't care about any of that. What I cared about was that Khaled wasn't playing my songs on the radio or in the clubs. I resented him. On Saturday nights, Khaled was the king of Club Krave. I'd be in there rolling on a bean—I was on ecstasy at the time—and when I wasn't dancing or tongue-kissing a random guy, I'd see other rappers sending drinks to the DJ booth to get Khaled to play their music. I couldn't force myself to choose that route. Instead, I sent out a message stating that I had a stack for whoever brought me his Terror Squad chain.

Dissing Khaled and everyone else was my attempt to get anything moving. I knew Khaled was not attempting to hold me back. On the few instances that we sliced it up, I could see he was sincere in his attempts at constructive criticism. I simply wasn't attempting to hear it.

However, burning bridges with the brass and attempting to intimidate niggas into submission did not serve me well. If anything, the extortion game served me poorly. I was more of a dissatisfied Miami resident than the mayor. The city was not rallying behind me. I was so frustrated that I didn't know how to act differently. I was exhausted and looked for any way to start a fire.

This rap garbage had to stop soon or I'd have to come up with another solution. I was now the father of a lovely baby girl, my daughter Toie, and her mother, Lastonia, was demanding money from me or she would file for child support. Lastonia and I never had a meaningful connection. She and I were always friends first and foremost. But at the time, we were bickering a lot.

My career was at a stop. The most success I saw was with ghostwriting. My collaboration with Trina had led to opportunities to work with a number of other female musicians. I wrote a song called

"Nookie" for E-Class's lady Jackie-O, which became a small hit and helped Poe Boy win a major label distribution deal. Then my big buddy Kane introduced me to a girl he discovered named Ashley Ross, with whom Gunplay and I began working closely.

I even had the pleasure to work with Angie Martinez, the Queen of New York Radio, at Audio Vision. Angie had just had a baby with Nokio from Dru Hill, and she still worked at Hot 97, so she needed help with her third album. I was delighted to do it for a small sum of money and a piece of publishing. Angie was very cool.

However, that small sum of money was insufficient to cover the bills. I was behind on my mortgage. I'd received a $30,000 advance from Slip-N-Slide and gave it all to my mother. She took it to Coldwell Banker and used it as a down payment on my first home, a two-story, three-bedroom home in a gated community in Pembroke Pines. The good news was that I was a homeowner at the age of 24. The bad news was that I was house poor. Soon, my mother was covering my mortgage and monthly car payment.

After signing with Slip-N-Slide, I expected the money to start rolling in. That's why I emptied the entire bag at home. But now I was broke, with no clear source of income on the horizon.

Living in the red will take its toll on you. I was heading back to Miami one night from a gig in Fort Myers. It was me, Gunplay, my friend P-Nut, and Ashley Ross. All four of us were intoxicated and fatigued. None of us wanted to drive or had any business doing so. But this event had only paid us $250, and we didn't want to spend it on a motel. The trip back to Miami was barely two and a half hours. Someone had to step up and take one for the team. And it was not going to be me.

"Nut, you ain't performing tonight," I told him, giving him the keys. "You're driving."

I dozed off in the passenger seat. Twenty minutes later, I awoke to the sound of my Escalade's tires striking the rumble strips. We were slipping off the freeway. I looked over to P-Nut, who was out cold.

"Nut!"

By the time he opened his eyes, it was too late. There was another car parked on the shoulder of the road, and our front passenger side collided with its rear end just as P-Nut cut the steering wheel, forcing my car to flip. We flipped two or three more times before coming to a stop upside down in the median.

My head was pounding and my ears were ringing, yet I could hear a hissing noise coming from the truck. The bitch was about to explode.

Gunplay, P-Nut, and Ashley wriggled their way out and ran. But my ass got jammed. My door was entirely caved in from the impact. I summoned Gunplay, who returned and assisted me in exiting via the front windshield.

When the cops arrived and inquired who was driving, there was silence. Nobody spoke a word. When they ran all of our licences, they returned and handcuffed me. Broward County had issued a warrant for my arrest. Lastonia or one of my neighbours had phoned the cops on me following one of our arguments. There weren't many young black niggas living in my gated community, so it didn't take much arguing to get one of them to contact the police.

I was placed in the back of a cruiser and driven to the local precinct. I would not be there long. Gunplay convinced his mother and his pregnant girlfriend to drive up from Miami and bail me out. They grabbed two cars so Gunplay's mother could put up her 1995 Toyota Celica as collateral.

As I sat in the holding cell, I kept shaking my head. I couldn't believe P-Nut had ruined my automobile and sent me to jail for it. Lastonia had charged my battery, and I couldn't believe it. I had just chatted to her the other day, and everything seemed fine. This must have happened a while ago.

But they were only the superficial issues that made me angry. I was deeply dissatisfied with my current situation in life. Suave House had not worked out. Slip-N-Slide was not working well. I had just nearly lost my life, and for what? Because I couldn't afford to spend the $250 I earned from performing at some shithole club in Fort Myers.

It's difficult to find buddies as dedicated as Gunplay. He pulled me out of the car. He summoned his men to help me out. But I could see he was ready to go away from music. The only reason he'd stayed with it so long was his devotion to me. Gunplay was with me wherever I was. This is how he is. But something has to change. The way things were going, it simply wasn't worth it.

Chapter 10

To say I wasn't where I wanted to be is an understatement. I had dropped out of college ten years ago to pursue music. Ten years of writing rap lyrics for other musicians. I've spent ten years sleeping in my car and on friends' floors. A decade of waiting for my turn and watching other niggas blow. And here I was. Still waiting.

The crackers at Atlantic were not the ones to pass me up. After his contract with Suave House expired, Block began working with Puff Daddy. Block knew Puff's girlfriend, Kim Porter, and she had introduced them. As I previously stated, Block knows everybody.

Puff had established a Bad Boy South section, signing 8-Ball and MJG as its first acts. Now he and Block are forming a group called Boyz N Da Hood. Boyz N Da Hood consists of Young Jeezy, Jody Breeze, Big Duke, and Big Gee. Puff and I met in passing on the set of Boyz N Da Hood's first music video, "Dem Boyz." But we met officially a few months later, when Block had Puff fly me up to New York to discuss my signing with Bad Boy South.

Jeezy has released his debut album and achieved stardom. He began to separate himself from the group, and Block and Puff were looking for a new fourth member for Boyz N Da Hood. Block was considering me, but he wasn't convinced. He was unsure if I would be a good fit. Block truly believed in me and saw me in the same light as Biggie or Jay-Z. I was an artist who was expected to be independent. He was considering having Gorilla Zoe replace Jeezy. However, he still wanted Puff to sign me.

Puff agreed with the notion that I was a down South Biggie. And that was the issue. That's the last thing he wanted. Puff had founded Bad Boy South to invest in the sound of the South. The game was evolving, and New York was losing its status as the dominant sound of hip-hop. So Puff wasn't looking for a rapper from the South who reminded folks of the best East Coast wordsmith to ever exist. That contrast alone put too much pressure on him.

I was becoming desperate. Every now and again, I think about how many times I've been asked if I'm a member of the Illuminati. I cannot help but laugh. Because, back then, if all I had to do was sell my mind, body, and soul for $100 million, I would have gladly accepted the offer. I'd have been a reptilian as a motherfucker.

However, there were no bargains with the Devil. This was the first time I recall looking to God to help me alter my life. This is when Steve Smoke convinced me to take communion at the Calvary Chapel in Fort Lauderdale.

Steve Smoke was Duece's landlord. Deuce lived at Alexander Towers, a fifteen-story seaside condominium complex in Hollywood, Florida. Steve was a sixty-something Caucasian man who owned nearly a hundred of these apartments.

I loved Steve, but he was a straight-up square. He would always stop by the flat to chat to Deuce about the back rent he owed or the odour of cannabis wafting out into the corridor. As soon as Steve stepped off the elevator, you could hear him complaining down the corridor.

"Ohhh, Deuce! "It smells like a skunk out here!"

Deuce got away with being a lousy tenant because Steve had other dealings with Ted at Slip-N-Slide. That was how Duece got connected to the apartment in the first place. Steve had heard via his connections with Slip-N-Slide that the new kid was causing all sorts of difficulties at the label. Steve referred to me as "the heathen" and was constantly curious about me.

Steve was a passionate disciple of Jesus Christ and an active member of Fort Lauderdale's evangelical megachurch, Calvary Chapel. Steve was encouraged as part of his Christian obligations to go out and bring in new believers. When Steve came up and saw all the cannabis, firearms, and hoes, he realised we were souls in need of salvation.

"Deuce, you have got to change your life," Steve stated. "I want you to join me at church on Sunday. If you can convince the heathen to accompany you, we can forget about last month's rent."

I wasn't interested in going, but I owed Deuce. My domestic violence case with Lastonia was handled when I agreed to attend weekly anger management classes, and Deuce joined me for everyone. Deuce had no reason to be there, but he was the only one who told the counsellor about his previous pimping and dope-selling experiences and how they had scarred him. I and the other niggas in there were just going through the motions to get this over with, but Duece enjoyed therapy. He got me through those anger management sessions, so I had to repay the favour and attend church with Steve Smoke.

Every week, Calvary Chapel accommodated over 20,000 worshippers. I had some experience with megachurches—E-Class, Pucci, and I used to ride around the city listening to Creflo Dollar's books on tape on prosperity theology—but being in one of these places was a spectacle. Unlike Creflo Dollar's World Changers Church, the Calvary Chapel's congregation was entirely composed of wealthy, white Florida residents. The only black faces I recall seeing were Donna Summer and her younger sister Mary Gaines Bernard, who were members of the church choir. Pastor Bob Coy built Calvary Chapel after years of working in the music industry, so they had a fantastic musical performance going on.

I went to the Calvary Chapel as a favour to Deuce, and Steve always took us out to dinner at Outback Steakhouse afterwards. When it was time to receive communion, Steve would always stare back at us, waiting for us to move to the front. By that moment, Deuce and I were generally ready to smoke and leave. Steve would simply shake his head.

But something kept bringing me back. I'd be sitting in church, and my phone would be exploding up in my pocket with all kinds of texts that could get me twenty-five to life. It made me think. Did I need to be saved? Were they communications from the Devil tempting me? After a few weeks of attending Sunday services, I eventually decided to take communion. I ate the wafer and drank the wine, praying that the lamb's blood would wash away my sins. When I turned back to Steve Smoke There were tears in his eyes.

Maybe it was a coincidence, but things did start to improve for me after that. I can't remember precisely when I took communion, but I know it was in November of 2005 when I received the phone call from Josh that transformed my life.

"Can you slide through C.O. 's house?" he inquired. C.O. was another artist signed to Slip-N-Slide as a member of the Tre+6 group. "I have this record here..." Please come through as soon as possible."

Josh received this beat CD from an Atlantic A&R representative for consideration on Trick's next album. Trick had already passed on this beat, as did T.I., Young Jeezy, and Juelz Santana, according to reports. But Josh believed this would be the one to turn things around for me. It was produced by The Runners, an Orlando-based duo. Josh inserted the CD and hit Play. It had an immediate impression on me.

Josh was not lying. This was a hit merely from the hook alone. I didn't even have to compose a chorus for this. As jaded as I was, I couldn't ignore what my ears were telling me. This beat felt like something. Josh and I sat in the studio listening for hours.

The next day, we drove up to Tampa, where I would be opening for Trina. During the drive, I had the instrumental playing on repeat. I lit a joint, took out a pen and notebook, and began writing. By the time we arrived at the location, I had finished a verse and wanted to try it out. I took the CD from the car and brought it inside.

At the end of my set, I handed the CD to Trina's DJ, Griot.

"I need you to play this track on here," I instructed him.

Opening acts have a difficult time capturing the audience's attention. You can trust me on that. I did this a lot. These folks came to see Trina, and I was the one they had to put up with to get there. But as soon as Griot hit Play on "Hustlin'," I had them eating out of my hand. Then I went for it.

I'd never seen the audience react to me like that before. Nobody at the show had ever heard "Hustlin'." It was not even a song. I had written a verse for an instrumental in the bus two hours before. Now there were a thousand people in front of me chanting "Every day I'm hustlin'" in chorus, as if it were a classic album they'd all heard a million times.

There was just one guy among the audience. He wore something dark green. I will never forget the look he gave me that night. I had never received one of those glances before. It was different. Something forceful. My song had reached this motherfucker's soul.

He hadn't simply heard "Hustlin'" via his ears. It had smacked him in the chest. In that moment, I realised that whatever I had just discovered with this song was where I needed to take my music in the future. I can still see his face quite well.

Josh smiled as I moved offstage.

"I think we got one, Fatboy," he said.

The following day, I went to Poe Boy Studios and composed two additional poems for "Hustlin'." After I put down the track, Josh and I went to see Ted.

Ted was probably even more annoyed with me than I was with Slip-N-Slide. I wouldn't be shocked if he was looking for someone to take my contract off his hands, just as he had taken me off Draper's. I had been slamming him and his label both personally and publicly, and now I was in his office pleading with him to put a sack behind my record.

"You know Atlantic's not supporting him any more, right?" Ted said. "So, if we want to promote this, we must do so with our own money. "Do you really believe in it?"

Josh replied, "Yes, absolutely." "One hundred percent."

Then he started afresh. Khaled was going crazy. He extended a four-minute tune into an hour, playing it back to back. He transformed the premiere of "Hustlin'" into something cinematic. That's when things changed.

The Rick Ross movement became a full court press from the moment Khaled unloaded the bombs on "Hustlin'". The entire city got behind me. Anyone who didn't know to move out of the path.

Khaled and every other radio DJ in Miami got in problems with their program management because they were playing the single so much. Within weeks, the same thing occurred in New York. Khaled had smuggled the tune to DJ Cipha Sounds, who was standing in for Funkmaster Flex at Hot 97 during the holidays. He kept playing "Hustlin'" back to back until he received an email from Ebro, Hot 97's music director, asking him what the fuck he was doing playing an unknown artist's song on loop. This was entirely against protocol.

Greg Street also got "Hustlin'" into circulation. He wasn't simply getting my music broadcast on V-103 in Atlanta. Greg was a cofounder of The Hittmenn DJs, a DJ coalition that served thirty areas in the South and Midwest, reaching millions of people.

The song was also extremely popular in the strip clubs. I witnessed it first hand at Tootsie's, Coco's, and Rollexx. But I kept hearing about this DJ who was blasting "Hustlin '" at Diamonds. Diamonds Cabaret was the upmarket establishment where all the baddest bitches danced. It was a little unfortunate for my taste. They did not allow you to wear shorts or smoke inside. So I had never been.

But this mysterious DJ had played "Hustlin'" so many times that he was suspended from the club. Then he returned and repeated the process, which resulted in his dismissal. Nobody on my team had been giving him money to play the music, and he hadn't contacted anyone.

People had been telling me about this DJ for weeks before I realised it was my little Haitian homie Sam Sneak. I met Sneak a few years ago at another club named MVP. He was a scrawny youngster who was too young to drink in the places he was spinning music at. I hadn't seen him in a while, but he was out here showing me all this affection and expecting nothing in return. The boy had a heart. I enjoyed it so much that I named him my official DJ from then on.

Meanwhile, E-Class, Gucci Pucci, and the rest of the Poe Boy street team—with a shout out to Johnny Boy—had taken over the streets of Miami. Earlier, I described E-Class as someone who can force his way into making things happen. That is undoubtedly true. But leaving it there would be a disservice to E. As "Hustlin'" took off. E-Class realised his true talent was in marketing and promotion. He captured the moment I was having and made it appear larger than life.

Every area of the city was covered in Rick Ross posters. E-Class purchased a cherry picker to ensure that I stood out from the others competing for eyeballs. There were picket signs. T-shirts. Rick Ross uses hot air balloons. Water bottles. Ten-foot-tall cardboard cutouts. When NBA All-Star Weekend came around, E-Class loaded thirty of those motherfuckers onto the side of a white diesel semi truck and drove it all the way to Houston.

You couldn't go scuba diving in Miami and not see my face. E-Class once discovered some waterproof board material and submerged them in water. E was on some other crap. His entire strategy was amazing.

Meanwhile, Ted was scheduling meetings with all of the major labels. All of them had come calling. Even the donkeys at Atlantic pretended to have first right of refusal. As if I had forgotten what happened a year ago. We had them travel to Miami and drive us to Prime One Twelve on Ocean Drive. We had ordered everything on the menu, including crab cakes, crab legs, jumbo fried shrimp with watermelon, lobster mac and cheese, bone-in rib eyes, and porterhouse steaks. Desserts included deep-fried Oreos and red velvet cake, as well as a plethora of takeout options. We maxed out their corporate credit cards.

Lyor Cohen was president of Warner Music Group, the parent company of Warner Bros. Records and Atlantic Records, which had recently combined. Lyor knew better than to send Craig and Mike back our way, so he asked Warner Bros.' chairman and CEO, Tom Whalley, to try to bring me on board.

This bidding war was taking place in the midst of the holidays, when the music industry typically closes for a few weeks. But this could not wait. Someone was going to sign Rick Ross. So Tom flew me, Ted, E-Class, and Josh out to his massive estate on Sunset Boulevard in Beverly Hills, where Tom and his team wined and dined us at a beautiful dinner party. Even the cook and maids tried to impress us. They made a big deal of it, and I have to give them credit; it was very remarkable.

Whalley was a cool guy. Fifteen years ago, he signed a teenage Tupac Shakur to Interscope and produced his debut album, 2Pacalypse Now. Kevin Liles, WMG's executive vice president, and Lorenzo "Irv" Gotti also attended the meal to finalise a deal with me. Irv Gotti founded Murder Inc. Records. He had recently been cleared of the money laundering accusations that had brought his company to its knees a year ago. He was working with Lyor and Kevin to relaunch Murder Inc. under Warner Bros., and signing me could be the label's big comeback.

Ted received a phone call just as we were boarding our aircraft back home. It was Shakir Stewart, Def Jam Records' Vice President of A&R.

"I just heard you are in California! Please do not sign the deal with Tom Whalley!"

"How the hell did you know we were out here?" Ted grumbled.

"Everybody knows!" Shakir said.

"Listen, we have not signed with anyone yet. We're just hearing everyone out. We're taking the red flight back to Miami now."

"Okay, great," Shakir said. "When you land, a plane will be waiting for you. I'll see you all in New York tomorrow morning."

Twelve hours later, I was in a conference room at Def Jam's headquarters in Manhattan. Shakir made a good initial impact. He had come up to New York from Atlanta, where he was headquartered, and I could tell he was on top of what was going on in southern hip-hop. He was the A&R for Def Jam signee Young Jeezy, whose debut album, Thug Motivation 101, produced success after hit. Shakir was on top of his game.

I got the same vibe from Def Jam's CEO, L.A. Reid, who said Shakir played him my song while they were vacationing together in St. Tropez. L.A. Reid's background was more R&B than hip-hop—he'd recently joined Def Jam following a legendary tenure with Babyface at La Face Records—but he appeared to understand and believe in what I was attempting to accomplish. I admired that he had been an artist as much as an executive. This was not some out-of-touch label executive attempting to cash in on the success of a single hit record.

I had a good vibe about these folks before. And then Jay-Z strolled into the room.

Jay-Z claimed he'd known about me for a while. His right-hand man, Memphis Bleek, had told him about me before "Hustlin'" took off. I met Bleek and State Property—a Philadelphia-based rap crew signed to Roc-A-Fella—a few years ago at Circle House. Bleek was working with Trick Daddy on a song titled "Round Here." But that day at Circle House, we had a cypher, and I battled the entire State Property crew for more than an hour. Beanie Sigel, Freeway, and The Young Gunz. I gave it to all the niggas. Apparently, I had made such an impact on them that they had informed Jay-Z.

Jay-Z and I had a connection that we didn't discuss throughout the meeting. We have never discussed it. But it's always been understood. It's the reason I've had more features from Jay-Z than any other artist. It's why Jay-Z shouted "Slip-N-Slide, Roc-A-Fella, One Umbrella" on the "Hustlin'" remix. It was because of Josh's close friend Versace Neal. Hov knew Neal from his previous life, and that connection fueled all of my early work with Roc-A-Fella. My cypher sessions with Kanye at Studio Center. My confrontation with State Property at Circle House. My brief appearance in the "Round Here" music video. All of this was made possible by a bond that existed before the music. And this made working with Jay-Z at Def Jam much more intriguing to me. Do you get what I mean when I say this shit goes deeper than rap?

All of the parts were present. Def Jam already felt like home. However, they would still have to be precise with the numbers because we already had a number of large offers on the table. That's when Hov delivered his final pitch.

"I just came over here as president," he told reporters. "And I want to finish this business, but I don't want to negotiate too much. So tell me what you need, and if it's fair to you and makes sense for Def Jam, I'll make it happen."

"Seven figures," I informed him.

"Done."

That is all she wrote. Rick Ross' bidding war was won.

Chapter 11

"Hustlin'" not only altered the trajectory of my career. It marked a new beginning for Miami's hip-hop scene. My colleagues' achievement came right after mine. Khaled had two successful singles, "Holla at Me" and "Born-N-Raised," which featured Pitbull, Trick Daddy, and myself and were produced by Cool & Dre and The Runners. Speaking of Dre, my homie stepped out from behind the decks with his own hit tune, "Chevy Ridin' High," on which I was featured. Then I returned and followed up "Hustlin'" with a Scarface-sampling second song called "Push It." Now everyone was eating. We dubbed our collective accomplishment "The Movement" and had no intention of slowing down.

When I planted my flag on the top of Club Rolexx for the "Hustlin'" music video, I felt like I had conquered the globe. But the triumphant feeling did not last long. Soon, fear set in. It had taken me so long to get here, and I had no idea how long this moment would endure. I'd watched Luke go from having everything to losing everything, and the notion of that happening to me was my biggest fear. I'd be in a casket before I appeared on an episode of Where Are They Now?

Fear kept me focused. I wasn't about to let this success pass me by. There was a lot of demand to follow up "Hustlin'" with something bigger, and I wasn't going to give in. So for the first nine months after I signed with Def Jam, I didn't spend a dollar of my advance. I did not spend any of my show money, either. I spent nine months doing two things. Getting money on the road and getting into the studio to record my debut album, Port of Miami.

I thought I'd cracked the code with "Hustlin'." It wasn't as if I had suddenly improved my rapping skills. If anything, I had dumbed down the lyrics to the song. I had been rapping circles around my peers for about a decade. But I couldn't find the appropriate production to fit the message. On my mixtapes, I was rapping over $500 beats or using industry instrumentals.

"Hustlin'" altered that. Producers recognized my potential and began giving me high-quality beats that suited the criteria. The production nailed the beauty and mysticism of South Beach with lyrics that alluded to the other side of the city, over the bridge. This combination became the driving force behind the sound of Port of Miami.

I was getting scheduled for a lot of shows. My rate increased from $5,000 to $15,000 to $25,000 within three months of "Hustlin'"'s release. That was a significant increase over the $250 shows I used to do, and I had no intention of leaving any money on the table. Each sack has to be retrieved. That meant I had to create an album on the go.

During a layover in Orlando, I caught up with The Runners and got three more beats from them. In Atlanta, I recorded the songs "Cross That Line" with Akon and "For Da Low" with Jazze Pha. In New York, I had my first studio session with Jay-Z for the "Hustlin'" remix. In Los Angeles, I met J.R. Rotem and took the beat for "Push It."

I was stretching my limits. I was on the road seven days a week, and on weekends, I was doing up to three gigs each night, with helicopters transporting me from one location to the next.

It wore me down. My voice cords were damaged, and my throat was killing me. I had doctors come to my hotel room to give me vitamin B12 shots, and I was sucking on ice cubes in the studio to get through my final Port of Miami gigs. At one point, I considered vocal cord surgery. You can hear how hoarse my voice had become throughout the CD. That was not a sound effect.

Jay-Z called after the numbers were in. "Hustlin'" had already been certified platinum earlier that summer, marking the first time an artist sold more than a million singles before releasing their debut album. I now have the number-one album in the country. Port of Miami sold 187,000 copies in its first week.

"It's an 187, nigga!" Jay-Z shouted. "We killin' 'em!"

A few weeks later, Jay-Z and I had a genuine celebration at the MTV Video Music Awards. He had his own personal runner deliver glasses of Ace of Spades to our seats at Radio City Music Hall. As we celebrated the Port of Miami's achievement, Ludacris and Pharrell played "Money Maker" on stage in front of us. At that moment, I realised how much of a difference there was between my success and Jay Z's. Jay was in a relaxed state. He was enjoying the awards ceremony and his bottle of champagne. I was having a good time as well, but the fear remained. Jay-Z could never rap another bar in his life and remain straight. I wasn't there yet. I still had a long way to go.

When the Port of Miami became Gold in November, I finally allowed myself a chance to regroup. It had been an entire year of relentless touring, recording, and marketing my CD. My girlfriend Tia gave birth to our kid, William Leonard Roberts III, weeks before I recorded "Hustlin'." Little Will. I was present for the delivery, but I haven't spent enough time with him since. I needed to fix that.

I felt blessed to be a father again. Toie was the apple of my eye, but I had always wanted a boy. My relationship with Tia was slightly more difficult. Tia and I had a good relationship for a while. If I were Biggie, she resembled a younger Faith Evans. However, Tia may be a hot mess. Not only did she fight with me, but she also fought with my mother and sister. She even was detained once for battling Lastonia. Tia already had two sons and a husband in prison, so we were never going to work out long-term. But I was trying to do the right thing by taking care of her and Lil Will. I purchased her a new Infiniti truck and paid her rent and bills.

In December, I purchased a three-story house with six bedrooms and seven bathrooms in Fayetteville, Georgia. My first multimillion-dollar home. As expected, Atlanta had emerged as the epicentre of hip-hop, and I wanted to be where business was thriving. After I got situated, I started working on my next album, Trilla.

I decided to approach this record a little differently. The Port of Miami was profoundly ingrained in my hometown. Now I want to go beyond 305. The title alone was a salute to my inspirations outside of Houston, combining Houston slang ("Trill") and Michael Jackson's Thriller. I also preferred to take my time with it. The majority of Port of Miami was written in the backseat of a conversion van between tour stops. The finished outcome was fantastic, but the creative environment was far from ideal.

I must have taken too long because by the end of 2007, Def Jam was growing impatient. It had been a year and a half since Port of

Miami's release, and the label wanted to put some numbers on the board. We had published a single called "Speedin'" but it did not do well. "Speedin'" was a great song, and we made a video for it where I raced speedboats with Diddy and Fat Joe. The problem was that I put R. Kelly on the record. R. Kelly had been charged on allegations of child pornography, and with his court date approaching, I believe many radio stations were reluctant to endorse "Speedin'" in case he was proven guilty. If I knew everything I know now, I probably wouldn't have included him in the song. But this was before Twitter and social media, and I was unaware of how sick he was.

I had another hit with T-Pain, which we all knew would be tremendous. However, the label intended to release Trilla shortly after the single, so the album had to be completed. Trilla had already been put back multiple times owing to sample clearance concerns, and Tony Draper had published Rise to Power, a collection of years-old unreleased work from my time at Suave House. Draper compensated me for that, but Def Jam wasn't pleased.

I was also ready to turn in Trilla. However, there was still something missing. Jay-Z had not put in his vocals. Hov had given me a verse for the "Hustlin'" remix, but I wanted us to have our own song. Jay-Z had resigned as Def Jam president, thus he was not working on their timetable. But he wasn't going to disappoint me either. He saved the day at the last minute.

Josh flew to New York and met with Jay-Z and Shakir at Battery Studios. That's when he performed Hov's "Maybach Music." I obtained the beat from J.U.S.T.I.C.E. League, a Tampa-based producing company. As soon as I heard the beat, I knew I wanted Jay to be on it. And I knew I wanted to call the tune "Maybach Music." What began as a song concept evolved into a six-part series and the name of my record label. It has now become synonymous with everything I do. When you think of Maybach, you think of Ricky Rozay.

The Mercedes-Benz Maybach had recently surpassed Rolls-Royce and Bentley as the world's most prestigious automobile, according to the Luxury Brand Status Index. I didn't know much about the list, but I knew the Maybach was the epitome of prestige.

I've owned a few Maybach coupes over the years, including the 57S and the S650 Cabriolet, but the back of a Maybach 62 is where you want to be. That's the extended sedan with reclining rear seats and an abundance of legroom. It has TV screens built into the back of the front seats. Writing desks that emerge from the armrests, similar to those found on aeroplanes. The back seat is where it's at. Because the truth is that a Maybach is not a car you buy to drive. It's a vehicle to be chauffeured in.

In my thoughts, the Maybach became a symbol of the kind of music I aspired to create. It indicated the amount of effort and attention to detail required to create something extraordinary. Music that sounded so exclusive and luxurious that someone could listen to it in their hoopty and feel transported to the back of a 62S.

The beat for "Maybach Music" sampled a cover of an old Beatles album, therefore J.U.S.T.I.C.E. League had to re-create the sample five times before Sony ATV and Paul McCartney approved its release. They then layered live instrumentation on top of the sample. The meticulousness that went into creating "Maybach Music" represented the entire notion behind it.

When Josh returned from New York, he told me that Hov freestyled his "Maybach Music" verse in one take, as I had seen him do when we recorded the remix to "Hustlin'." He also mentioned that Hov had given us something more to go with his verse. These two Australian supermodels, Jessica Gomes and Cheyenne Tozzi, had been hanging out in the studio while he was recording, and they had some gorgeous accents. Hov sent them into the booth and instructed them to talk about Maybach.

"What is this?"

"Maybach Music."

"I like this Maybach Music."

"Sweeeeet..."

They both laughed. That's how the classic "Maybach Music" drop came about. It's been more than ten years since that studio session, and I'm still not tired of hearing it. There is something timeless about the discussion. A few years later, Jay-Z told me something amusing about it. By then, I was using it in every song I released. I started giggling as soon as he said it. Hov does not forget anything.

I am still waiting for you to thank me for that.

Chapter 12

I possess the gift of foresight. I can see the various outcomes of a situation. Every potential consequence. However, this does not always happen. Some storms arrive unexpectedly.

There'd be no sophomore slump. Trilla was another number one, selling just under 200,000 copies in its debut week. My track with T-Pain, "The Boss," debuted in the Top 20 of the Billboard Hot 100 and became my second certified platinum record following "Hustlin'."

Things were going pretty well. The label was pleased. The fans were pleased. The money was building up. I was dating Foxy Brown, and our relationship was amazing. I'd had feelings for Foxy ever since I first heard her sing "Touch Me, Tease Me" in 1996. I met her on the set of DJ Khaled's "Out Here Grinding" video that summer, and we got along well.

Aside from a tiny legal issue, I did not have much to complain about. At the beginning of 2008, I was arrested in North Miami following a traffic stop. I had been accused of carrying a concealed firearm and possessing marijuana. The arrest was nothing to worry about. The cannabis charge had already been dropped, and the gun charge would follow shortly thereafter. I had a carry permit, but due to an oversight, it was listed as suspended.

The case was going to be dismissed. The only thing that concerned me was when my lawyer learned that my case had been sent to the police department's gang task team. During his deposition, the arresting officer was told that it was because of my supposed ties to the Carol City Cartel group.

"Why was this case assigned to the gang task force?"

"Because your client claims affiliation with the Carol City Cartel and other known gang members."

"Where did you get that from?"

"Other detectives."

"Is that pulled out of the vast universe, or do you have something definitive?"

"I think there is some literature or video on YouTube that you can pull up for yourself."

I had to proceed with extra caution. I wore a "Boobie Boys" T-shirt in the "Hustlin'" video. Then I released a documentary called M-I-Yayo, which ranked the top ten dope dudes in Miami history. I was basically ridiculing law police.

I was still too connected to the streets to act recklessly. So I was conscious of my movements this time. I knew that something from my history could be dredged up and exploited against me. I never imagined it could be what it turned out to be.

Halfway through the summer, one of my homies called and said there was something I wanted to see. A photo of myself from a Florida Department of Corrections graduation ceremony appeared on a website. I was clothed in a correctional officer uniform and shook hands with a middle-aged white woman named Marta Villacorta. Marta was the warden of the South Florida Reception Center, a state prison in Doral.

I'm bringing this up now, rather than earlier in the book, since my time as a correctional officer became a significant part of my story. Prior to this time, I thought of it in the same way that I did when I used to wash cars or when my mother got me a job with the Department of Health delivering medicine to individuals who were too sick to leave their house.

When I dropped out of Albany State and moved home, I needed to find work. I was making money, so it wasn't so much about the money as it was about having something to tell my mother about what I was doing with my life. If I wasn't in college, I would have had to find a job. Those were the restrictions if I wanted to reside in her home.

I really wanted to work at the docks. I wanted to be a longshoreman. I used to bug Gino, my tattoo artist and good buddy, to introduce me to his younger brother Kano. Kano was part of a Haitian crew known as the R.O.C., which stood for "Rich Off Cocaine." They were infamous for carrying out massive heists at the Port of Miami. They'd be notified of inbound cargo ships bringing in some kilos, and things could proceed in one of two ways. Either Kano and his team would hijack the freighters at sea, strip everyone naked, throw their phones into the ocean, and force someone to hang up the goods. Alternatively, they would wait until the goods were off the docks. Kano and his team would then stop the smugglers and loot them while masked as undercover police agents. They'd be driving unmarked Crown Victorias equipped with strobe lights and everything. This was high-level piracy.

I wanted to be the inside man at the docks, but you needed a union connection to get the position. I'd drop clues at Gino to get him to introduce me to Kano. Gino also did bespoke airbrushing, and one time I brought in a pair of Timberlands and $200, telling him I wanted "Rich Off Cocaine" written on them. The boots turned out fantastic, but Gino didn't take the bait/bribe to connect me with Kano. He did not want either of us to get into any more trouble than we were already in.

That's when I applied for a position with the Florida Department of Corrections. I already knew a few niggas who worked as corrections officers. It was a common occupation for huge, mean ex-football players. It was also an easy job to get, given that Florida has one of the highest incarceration rates in the country. Being a CO is not a career for someone who has always wanted to work in law enforcement.

I spent my first six months in the Department of Corrections' basic recruit training program. During the 540-hour course, I took multiple-choice questions, completed obstacle courses, and learned first aid and CPR.

The main campus of the South Florida Reception Center is a violent place, but they don't throw you to the wolves immediately. As a Level I correctional officer, I was posted to a watchtower on the prison's South Unit. The South Unit housed six hundred convicts, the majority of whom were elderly or unwell. After a few months in the tower, I was promoted, which meant I could accompany these guys to the hospital ward and wait while they recovered from various surgeries and procedures. As you might expect, these detainees were not particularly troublesome.

The goal was to get transferred to the main unit. When I went over there, this correctional officer thing was going to be a lick. The income was still bad—my initial salary was less than $25,000—but this was where you could make money off the books by bringing in pot or allowing niggas to finger their girls during visitation. The main unit was where I would meet niggas I knew. Or niggas who Mike or Boobie knew. They both had extensive contacts and influence in the penitentiary system. They really did have connections everywhere. The Fire Department. The telephone company. The police.

For a while, I tried to do the work to the best of my ability. I arrived on time. I tracked my hours. I wrote the reports. But that didn't last very long. People don't realise how uneventful prison life can be, whether you're an inmate or a CO. I'd never been so bored in my life. I started smoking pot before I got inside. Then I'd just sit there, waiting for the days to end. I'd glance over the barbed wire fence and picture a different existence awaiting me on the other side. Something better than this. Something exceptional.

I never got to the main unit. I believe some of the higher-ups were aware that I knew folks over there. My managers were not interested in relocating me to the main campus, and once I learned this, I concluded that the employment was done. So I quit. That was pretty much it.

However, the blogs spun this tale as if I were an undercover cop or confidential informant. I could not believe it. The attack on my character took me completely off guard.

There were many people who knew about it. I had never made an effort to conceal it. I used to pick up Gunplay after work and go to Earl's studio while still in my uniform. If anything, Gunplay was envious that his rap sheet prohibited him from landing a government job with perks. I believe he was still working at the AT&T store at the time.

Anyone close enough to me to be aware of this would know better than to doubt my credibility. No girl had ever denied me pussy, and no nigga had ever teased me about my job as a correctional officer.

Because the instant anyone got close enough to smell the cloth from which I was cut, they knew I was ready to depart.

This had to come from someone who was near enough to know the truth but still wanted to sabotage me. And the public didn't know any better than to believe whatever story the websites told them. Before I had a chance to address the problem, one of the blogs published a piece featuring a statement from me questioning the legitimacy of the photo.

"My life is completely real. These online hackers are posting an image of my face from when I was a teenager in high school on other people's bodies. If this garbage was true, don't you think they'd have more information, like dates and all?"

I hadn't mentioned that. I had not communicated with any media outlets regarding the situation. I'm not sure if they made up the phrase or if someone in my camp issued it on my behalf. But it did not originate from me. What I do know is that those sites eventually took those pieces down. They did not stand by their report.

But that doesn't matter because this is when I made my mistake. Instead of correcting the record right away, I went on to deny the claim in subsequent interviews. The scenario had quickly unravelled, and I was made to feel as if I had something to hide. Everything had been going so well, and suddenly everyone was screaming I had been exposed, putting my entire career in peril. I'd never seen a meme before, and all of a sudden I was seeing altered images of my head on movie posters for RoboCop and Big Momma's House.

I should've taken a moment to assess the situation and respond accordingly. Instead, I became caught up in the drama and reacted quickly. When another website dredged up my personnel information a week later, everything became much worse. I wasn't only being labelled an imposter. I was a liar, too. That bit was actually correct. I had only myself to blame for that. The worst part about lying is that once you've said it, you have to stick to it. For a while, that's what I did.

The entire rap scene was in a frenzy over whether Rick Ross was a phoney. Everyone had an opinion. Maino said he was disappointed with me. Ludacris, Fabolous, and Fat Joe came to my defence. Even Freeway Rick came out of the woodwork to claim I stole his name.

I was fuming. Even toward those who were aware of the situation and supported me. Why the fuck were these niggas asked to weigh in on this in the first place? The scenario made me realise the power of blogs and how they can carry a narrative further. I was being used for clickbait. Money was being earned at the expense of my livelihood.

My frustrations erupted during the 2008 Ozone Awards in Houston. Trilla won Album of the Year that night, but I was unable to enjoy it. I was in battle mode. When my group came with DJ Vlad, one of the bloggers who had been pouring gasoline on the fire, he suffered a pounding on behalf of everyone who had been slandering my reputation. Broken nose. Broken eye socket. Seven stitches. The incident would cost me $300,000 in settlement. I believe that night, all parties involved learnt the true cost of doing business.

I would never admit it out loud, but I was in a dark place. The environment around me had become strained, putting a strain on my relationships. My affair with Foxy fizzled away. I had a falling out with E-Class and sacked him as manager. I cut all relations with Slip-N-Slide again.

They weren't the only ones who quit my tight group that year. In November, I received a call informing me that Shakir Stewart had committed suicide. He shot himself in his Georgia home, leaving behind a fiancée and two children. He was thirty-four years old.

I could not believe it. And I wasn't sure what to believe. There were so many insane rumours flying around. That Shakir had been murdered. He had been leading a double life. It screwed me up.

With Shakir gone, I had no idea what my future at Def Jam would be like. Jay-Z departed as the label's president the previous year. As much as I admired and respected L.A. Reid, his help and advice were never as hands-on as Shakir's. Shakir had been the glue that kept everything together. When Ted and I disagreed, he would step in to mediate and make things right. He was the best A&R I had ever worked with. He possessed a unique ability to connect the sounds of the streets with the mainstream. That was not going to be an easy replacement.

Chapter 13

The week Trilla came out, I heard 50 Cent say my name for the first time.

At the time, 50 was feuding with Fat Joe and released a video mocking Joe's new album, The Elephant in the Room, which sold poorly in its first week of availability.

"That's when you realise you aren't relevant. When fresh performers like Ricky Ross, the Boss, come out looking great with a number one album. He's from the same little area in Miami, but he shouldn't stand next to that fat piece of shit because you know how I am. You know how I am, right?"

50 hadn't shown his hand just yet, but I recognized a disguised threat when I heard it. This was his MO. For years, 50 had started feuds with artists and then went after anyone supported them. And it worked. He had defeated every opponent to date. 50 has already utilised his dispute with Fat Joe to begin dissing Khaled. He was keeping it nice with me for the time being, congratulating me on Trilla's achievement, but I knew if he was coming after Khaled, it was only a matter of time until he came for me. 50 was just down the line.

I didn't get back to 50 until the beginning of 2009. Coming off the correctional officer issue, the last thing anyone wanted was a fight with 50 Cent. We already had enough issues, and 50 would have all the ammunition he required. I was informed that it would be self-sabotage.

But I saw the issue differently. For six months, I had been on the defence. Every time DJ Vlad's wig was split, another donkey took his place. I was playing whack-a-mole. However, 50 Cent's story was rather different. This was the most powerful bully in the rap game. If I sat his ass down, all the sceptics would be silenced. It would be like chopping off the head of a snake.

I put 50 on notice with a few bars on a song called "Mafia Music," in which I mentioned recent claims that he attempted to burn down his house while battling for child support with his ex-girlfriend.

"Really?" Khaled stated when he first heard "Mafia Music." "This is how we're coming?"

Khaled had recently been named president of Def Jam South, taking over Shakir's prior position as my A&R and point person at the label. While he appreciated me defending him, this was not the way he wanted to start his new job. Khaled is a man of peace. "Mafia Music" represented a declaration of war.

50 responded a few days later with "Officer Ricky." This fool has the guts to throw my credibility into doubt. His entire career revolved around him getting shot nine times. Where I came from, getting shot was not something to celebrate. We were the niggas doing the shooting.

50 was very fugazi. He had never reached the same level as me on the streets. The niggas he grew up with in Queens? They were the kind of niggas I gave bricks to on consignment when I was eighteen, and they paid me back every cent ahead of time. 50 wasn't even enough. He would have been the thug who filled up my truck with gas before I left town. Fifty Cent would have bought me air fresheners.

But I knew 50 would take the same road he did. It was the simplest path in front of him. What surprised me was how weak the song was. "Mafia Music" was more than simply me firing off a few casual bullets to the 50s. It was some of my best rapping so far. There's no chorus. Only four and a half minutes of straight bars. So I was anticipating 50 Cent, who damaged Ja Rule's career on "Back Down." However, "Officer Ricky" sounded like "Candy Shop" 2.0. The music was dreadful.

"Yeah, I heard it," I told Angela Yee in a radio appearance with Shade 45 the following day. "I knew that couldn't be the solution. Tell me he is joking. We're all going to pretend we didn't hear that nonsense. We're going to give you another 48 hours. Take your time. Return to the lab and come up with something different.

50 recognized he couldn't compete with me bar by bar, so he changed his strategy. He shifted focus away from the music and began attacking me with a bizarre series of publicity stunts. There were cartoons featuring "Officer Ricky". In sketch comedy videos,

he wore a curly perm wig. I believed I was hallucinating the first time I saw him wearing that crap. This nigga was ocky!

I may have gotten under 50's skin by discussing his troubles with his baby mommy, because he took off with that theme. I wasn't burning down my house, but I didn't have the cleanest yard either. I was in the midst of my own custody struggle. I had just been deposed in Broward County Family Court. 50 pounced on it. He contacted Tia and paid her a little money to go out and trash me in interviews. Then he bankrolled her so she could publish a book about our relationship.

50 was currently working on his own book. He was drafting one with Robert Greene, the author of The 48 Laws of Power. I had read Greene's book and did not agree with all of its principles. I did not favour stealing credit for other people's work, seeking a scapegoat to blame for mistakes, or appearing as a friend to adversaries. But I was obviously putting some of its ideals into effect. Strike the shepherd, and the sheep will scatter. Stir the waters to attract fish. The mirror effect both disarms and infuriates. And completely crush your enemies.

After getting everything he could out of Tia, 50 acquired a sex tape of Lastonia and leaked it online. I cannot say I was completely surprised. Lastonia was my homegirl, yet she got herself into these situations. The only thing that troubled me was how it was going to affect Toie. I wanted to keep her and Lil Will safe from all of this. When 50 began publishing photos of himself, Tia, and Will together at Floyd Mayweather's mansion, a line had been passed.

They say desperate people do desperate things, and 50 appeared to get desperate quickly. When I saw he was under pressure and had to resort to all this bizarre shit—the fucking donkey was pursuing Khaled's mother at one point—I began to relax. I'd been on the defense for so long that I'd forgotten how much I loved putting the squeeze on a nigga. That is when I became the aggressor.

This was around the time that I began shooting a lot of visuals with my videographer Spiff TV. We shot one for "Mafia Music" and then headed up to New York to shoot another for a follow-up song called "Kiss My Pinky Ring Curly." I wanted people to understand what a square 50 was and how I was more credentialed in his city than he was. Torch had the Bronx behind me. Kano was following me from Brooklyn. 50 would never come to Miami like that.

Then I enlisted Game, Ja Rule, and Fat Joe, all of whom had their own issues with Curly, to contribute to a remix of "Mafia Music" and take shots at him. Then I staged a faux funeral for 50 people in the music video for "In Cold Blood."

Spiff was ahead of the curve when it comes to shooting videos with DSLR cameras. We began releasing new content on WorldStarHipHop every other day, and rappers approached me, asking how I got Def Jam to pay for all of these music videos and vlogs. But the label had not put up a dime for those. Spiff shot them guerilla-style on the move. Every rapper soon had a shooter following them around with a Canon 5D.

Meanwhile, 50 kept squandering all of his money. I'm not sure how much he spent on Tia's book, but that sex tape with Lastonia would cost him $5 million in an invasion-of-privacy case. I was approached by people claiming to have dirt on 50 and G-Unit, but I couldn't bring myself to pay for hearsay. So I just kept my foot on his neck with the music and vlogs, mocking him for how he dressed and his hideous artificial teeth.

Things had been tight for a long time, but it eventually started to get entertaining. I was a hip hop student. It was amazing to be a part of a rivalry like this, with the entire game in a frenzy. I even tried to boost the ante by calling out 50's big friend Eminem, but he didn't take the bait.

After his album was delayed, 50 became quieter. He had been attempting to recreate the sales battle he had with Kanye West a year earlier. He'd spent all of his money and time attempting to get me out in the hopes that it would boost his faltering career and generate buzz for his album. The problem was that releasing sex tapes and shooting photos with my son didn't improve his music. Every single he tried to release was a dud. Interscope had already dropped Lloyd Banks and Tony Yayo, so 50 had to start from scratch if he wanted his label to give him a release date.

I had a secret weapon that I kept hidden while Woodface and I were arguing. I had something he couldn't afford with his money from the 1950s. It wasn't a dossier with his dirty laundry. I had a fantastic album waiting in the wings. When my back was against the wall, I created the best music of my career. And I was going to drop it when the pressure was at its peak and the lights were the brightest. That's when I drove the final nail into Curly's coffin. That's when I released Deeper Than Rap.

Chapter 14

Deeper than Rap, in the words of my brother DJ Khaled, was "Another One." But this triumph was particularly delicious. My third number-one album had arrived in the midst of difficulty. I'd endured my punishment, but I'd come out on top. When the chips were down and the chances were stacked against me, I did not roll up into a ball and hide. I stood tall and fought. Everyone who had written me off had to backtrack.

I felt bulletproof. That sensation motivated me to rename my fourth album after my former nickname. Teflon Don. But before I could get started, I needed to call out my brothers who were with me when I was Tef. I needed to introduce the world to the Three C's.

The group had been on the back burner since my solo career took off, but with the success of Deeper Than Rap, I felt more assured about my future. Nobody was taking me out of here.

In my absence, Gunplay and Torch had been raising the Triple C's banner and doing gigs together. But Triple C's identity was a three-headed monster. I wanted to get back to making music with Gunplay and Torch, but I didn't want to abandon them once I got back to working on my own shit. I wanted Triple C's to be capable of functioning independently of me. That is when I introduced Young Breed to the group.

Breed was 10 years younger than me, but his elder brothers were street niggas that I knew growing up. Breed had been rapping for a while and was well-known in Miami, despite his youthful age. He was already a member of another group named Piccolo, but he had been working in the studio with Gunplay and Torch, both of whom recommended him highly. The more I learned about Breed, the more I believed he would be an excellent fit for Triple C's. When you mentioned Carol City Cartel, the image that came to mind was of him. Whereas Torch was from the Bronx and Gunplay was a mash-up of Miami, New York, Jamaica, and Puerto Rico, Breed was a straight-up gutter Carol City nigga with dreadlocks and gold chains talking about Chevys and choppers.

I also wanted Triple Cs to have their own representation outside of my management. So I elevated Geter K from muscle to manager. Geter was one of Torch's Bronx homies, and he had earned his keep hanging out with us. Geter was a Gladiator. He nearly punched Vlad's eye out of his head at the Ozone Awards. That wasn't the only time Geter's hands prompted me to sue, but Triple C's was a rough-and-tumble group in need of forceful management. Geter fits the bill.

I had just delivered three straight number-one albums, so Def Jam was giving me exactly what I wanted. And I planned to launch my own imprint, Maybach Music Group, with the first release being a Triple C's group album called Custom Cars & Cycles.

We had a lot of fun creating Custom Cars & Cycles, so it was upsetting when the album failed. Following Jay-Z's departure and Shakir's death, Def Jam was going through a transition phase, and the release slipped through. That was unfortunate because the CD was well received and people appeared to be having fun with the group. People didn't dislike Triple Cs. The record simply wasn't advertised properly. Regardless, I felt like I did what I set out to do. I had shone a light on my brothers, putting them in a position to triumph.

Before I could begin working on Teflon Don, I wanted to help one more old pal. At the beginning of 2010, I received a call from Kanye West's management inviting me to Hawaii. Kanye was locked up in Avex Honolulu Studios working on something. He had reserved all three of the studio's recording rooms for 24 hours a day, until further notice.

Kanye had travelled to Hawaii to get away. It served as a getaway from his domestic issues. He had found safety there a year and a half before, after his mother died. This getaway inspired his fourth album, 808s and Heartbreak. Kanye had travelled to Hawaii after an incident at the 2009 MTV Video Music Awards. He interrupted Taylor Swift's acceptance speech to declare that the honour should have gone to Beyoncé. He received a lot of heat for it. Even President Obama labelled him a jackass.

It had been eight years since I last saw Kanye. I had gotten him on "Maybach Music 2," but it was done remotely. We hadn't been in the studio together since our cyphers at Studio Center in 2002. A lot has changed since then. For the both of us.

I wasn't sure what to anticipate from our reunion when Pucci, Spiff, and I arrived at our Hilton hotel on Waikiki Beach. But once we arrived at the studio, I realised this wasn't going to be my regular guest verse. The first thing I saw were all the signs Kanye had posted on the walls.

I had no idea what tweeting was, but I was aware that something unusual was happening here. Kanye had flown in a slew of rappers, producers, and songwriters to work on this project. Legendary beat makers include No I.D., Pete Rock, and DJ Toomp. Young superstars in the making include Nicki Minaj, Kid Cudi, and Big Sean.

This was the routine. Every day would begin at 10:00 a.m. with breakfast at Kanye's crib on Diamond Head. Sometimes we arrived before he did. Kanye would still be in the studio from the night before. He had two full-time chefs there, serving up French toast with flambéed bananas while everyone chatted about what we had worked on the night before and what we planned to do at the studio today. These were Knights of the Round Table talks.

During one of those breakfasts, Kanye and I got to talking about Pusha T. Pusha was one half of the Virginia rap group Clipse, who had recently released their third album, Till the Casket Drops. Kanye had a song named "Kinda Like a Big Deal" on the album, but he never worked on it. He'd recorded his verse for a T.I. song called "On Top of the World," but it ended up being featured on the Clipse song instead.

So Kanye did not know Pusha T. But I did, and I told you my judgement on him. Someone like Pusha T might be a huge asset in this context, and I suggested Kanye look into his label issue as well. I got them on the phone, and the rest became history. I'd already left Hawaii by the time Pusha arrived, but he got a few placements on the record, and Kanye eventually signed him to G.O.O.D. Music.

After breakfast, Kanye would go to the YMCA and play some pickup basketball. Spiff and I would frequently skip the gym. We'd take our little Kia rental car and explore the island. We'd go to

met Kanye in New York near the end of his album, he had a fresh version of the song. His engineer Mike Dean had added a mean guitar solo breakdown at the end, which Kanye wanted me to come in after. But he asked me to write a new stanza. He disliked the one I had done in Hawaii.

"I know that you can do something better than that," I heard him say.

That is what he said. Then he stood up, turned around, and left the studio.

It was a good thing he departed. I needed a minute to digest what had just transpired. In all my years, no one had ever asked me to change a verse. Even when I was a nobody ghostwriting for much bigger musicians, no one ever said anything like that.

I was astonished, but not insulted. I wasn't pissed. That astonished me, too. I knew Kanye had not said something to offend me. He was pushing me in the same manner he had pushed everyone else in Hawaii. In the same way, he was pushing himself to accomplish something much larger. So, the ball was in my court. I had two options: disregard his request or accept his challenge. I opted for the latter, and two hours later I had another poem. Many of my admirers consider it the pinnacle of my career.

When I returned from Hawaii, I got started on Teflon Don. Working alongside Kanye and his tutor No I.D. motivated me to improve my production value. I made sure to obtain beats from both of them—Ye gave me "Live Fast, Die Young" and No I.D. gave me "Tears of Joy." Then DJ Clark Kent of the famed Supermen DJs emerged from his semi-retirement to present me with Teflon Don's debut record, "Super High." Meanwhile, J.U.S.T.I.C.E. League was busy working on the third chapter of "Maybach Music." It would take some time to outdo all of the arrangements and live instruments from the second instalment.

I had all these renowned producers engaged in Teflon Don, so it was amusing when two beats from an unknown youngster kicked off the record. I believe Lex Luger completed "MC Hammer" and "B.M.F." in ten minutes.

I was at Central Station in Atlanta for the "O Let's Do It" music video shoot. "O Let's Do It" was Gucci Mane's protégé Waka Flocka Flame's breakout single. In his mentor's absence—Gucci having been arrested again—Waka took up the 1017 Brick Squad torch and ran with it. He'd gotten Puff, Fabolous, and me to work on the remix of "O Let's Do It."

Waka had another record that was doing well on the set that day. "Hard in da Paint." It wasn't your standard radio-friendly single. There was nothing nice about it. It sounded sinister, and Waka's barking added to the ominous atmosphere. I knew I could do something tough over that beat.

I had Spiff find out who the producer was for "Hard in da Paint" so I could record my own version. It turned out to be Lex Luger, an eighteen-year-old from Virginia. Waka found him on Myspace and invited him to Atlanta, where he spent six months hammering out beats on a TR-808 drum machine assembly line.

Lex handed over more than fifty beats, which Spiff narrowed down to about twenty that he felt I'd enjoy. Lex's beats sounded similar, yet he had a distinct sound. This collection of beats inspired "MC Hammer" and "B.M.F."

I was going through the Hollywood Hills when I came up with the name "MC Hammer." I had travelled to Los Angeles to shoot the music video for "Super High." As I was leaving the set to return to my hotel, Stiff began running over Lex's rhythms. I was so high on the drive. I was smoking California's finest—my favourite strain, P.R. 80—and as I glanced out the window at all the mansions and sports cars, all I could think about was how MC Hammer lived in the 1990s.

I was very close with Puff at the time. It was rumoured that Puff had joined my team as manager, although there was never a formal agreement in place. Basically, Puff and I were partying a lot back then, and it resulted in a lot of fantastic songs and commercial partnerships (I became an ambassador for his Cîroc vodka).

I flew to New York to meet with Puff and outline my game plan. Teflon Don wasn't set to be released for a few months, but I wanted to hit the streets now. I had a sense Lex Luger would become the most sought-after producer in the industry, and I wanted to be at the forefront of that sound. So I wanted to release The Albert Anastasia EP as a prelude to Teflon Don and a sign of things to come.

Puff went nuts when I performed "MC Hammer" for him at Daddy's House Studios in Midtown Manhattan. He was practically asking me to let him put a poem on there. But he despised that I was going to put it on Albert Anastasia. He was dead set against it. This song was really popular. I couldn't just upload it for free to Datpiff and LiveMixtapes. It would become lost in the sea of free music that flooded the internet every day.

Puff Daddy has been as essential an adviser to me throughout my career as Tony Draper, Jay-Z, or any other legend from whom I've been fortunate to learn the game. However, just because someone is a terrific consultant does not imply you should follow all of their recommendations. I realised it was time for me to feed the streets. Deeper than Rap received tremendous accolades and helped me get a lot of new fans. I was finally gaining respect as a lyricist. But I hadn't heard an anthem like "Hustlin'" or "The Boss" in a long time. Songs like "Maybach Music 2" were exquisite works of art, but they weren't destroying the clubs. "MC Hammer" was supposed to change that, and I planned to release it on the eve of Memorial Day weekend. I planned to set the tone for the entire summer.

On the morning of the Albert Anastasia EP's release, I recorded a song for the mixtape at the last minute: "B.M.F." Spiff played me "B.M.F.", another Lex Luger beat, one night in Washington, DC, while we were lounging on Khaled's tour bus. I zoned out to it for a while and ultimately began mumbling a hook, which Spiff would transcribe on his Blackberry for us to explore when we returned to the studio. When Spiff received an iPhone, we began making voice memos, but that was our creative process at the time.

I didn't return to the beat until the night before its release, when I finished writing my verses to it. But I didn't put them down that night. I'd been travelling hard, and my vocal cords were once again scorched. I tried drinking lemon honey tea and giving it a go, but it didn't work.

The following morning, I decided to give it one more attempt. My engineer, E-Mix, needed to start mixing and mastering Albert Anastasia if we were going to release it that night. My marketing and promotions wizard, Lex Promo, required the final track list before he could begin making CDs and hitting the streets. And I had to leave to catch a flight elsewhere. There was no more time left. I got into the booth and said "B.M.F." in one take.

The insane shit about "B.M.F." is how Styles P ended up there. I had been discussing doing a record with Styles, but not over one of Lex Luger's beats. I was hoping we'd do some East Coast, Yonkers, L.O.X. kind things. Not an Atlanta trap. Styles' verse in the song is so powerful that I wish I could take credit for recognizing the vision. But the truth is that it was a complete accident.

Lex Luger sent Spiff this batch of beats, which were all numbered. He did not name each one individually. After Spiff completed his A&R chores and selected the ones he felt I might enjoy, he began circulating the remainder to the other artists he was working with at the moment. Styles was one of these musicians. When Styles P returned a verse on the "B.M.F." rhythm, Spiff recognized his error. He had mistakenly sent him one of the beats intended for me.

"All of these got the same 808s," Spiff stated. "I could just find another one to put his vocals on."

"Nah, but he killed that," I explained. "Let's keep him there."

That's how the "B.M.F." rhythm resurfaced on my radar shortly before the release of Albert Anastasia. We had sort of forgotten about it until Styles sent Spiff his poem. That reminded me of how difficult it was and how I'd come up with this hook that would have all the dope dudes in a frenzy.

The way the streets reacted to "B.M.F." Memorial Day weekend in 2010 was the most similar to how it felt when I originally released "Hustlin'."

I don't think the song charted particularly high on the Billboard charts, but it didn't have to. It was a hymn for the streets.

The anticipation for Teflon Don was high, and I was almost ready to drop it. However, something was still missing. Once again, I was waiting for Jay-Z's vocals.

I had gotten Jay-Z to appear on Teflon Don's second hit, "FreeMason." However, when Khaled travelled to New York to finish mixing the record, he was unable to obtain the files from Jay's sessions. Guru, Jay-Z's engineer, informed Khaled that the hard disk used for the session had broken.

Khaled began to panic. He didn't have a close relationship with Jay-Z at the time, but he began blowing up his phone. Jay-Z did not react right away, so Khaled began contacting everyone on his phone who knew Jay-Z. I wasn't there for any of this, but according to Khaled, he was lying down in the middle of Times Square, texting Jay-Z's phone repeatedly, imploring him to re-lay his verse. Khaled is nuts.

But Hov always maintains it 100% and comes through. He finally texted Khaled back, saying he was on vacation in the Hamptons and would recreate the verse as soon as he returned to the city. But Teflon Don needed to be turned in the next day if we wanted to drop it on July 20, which had already been pushed back twice. So Jay-Z had his engineer come to his Hamptons home with all of the studio equipment so that he could finish the song for me before the deadline.

Khaled was still out of breath from the entire ordeal when he called to inform me what had transpired. Khaled knows me well, and he knew better than to bring up this issue until it was resolved. When I'm in the mood for an album, I don't want to hear about such nonsense.

"My nerves are so bad right now," he said. "But I finished it, Rozay." "I finished it."

"I know you don't think I believe that story, Khaled," I shared with him. "Who the fuck drops Jay-Z's hard drive on the train?"

"You don't believe me?" Khaled said. "You can ask Guru!"

"If anything, Jay probably heard me body my verse on there and it made him want to redo his," I claimed.

I didn't really think that. I was simply fucking with Khaled. I advised him he should definitely go to the doctor because he appeared stressed. He informed me that he had already seen numerous.

With "Free Mason" completed, my fourth record was ready to go. When it was released a few weeks later, the reception was unequivocal. Teflon Don was my magnum opus.

Chapter 15

The critical acclaim that Teflon Don received was greatly welcomed. However, no album review can compare to the sensation of hearing someone say your music helped them get through a difficult time. That's the ultimate praise. Especially if that person is Lil Wayne.

Wayne contacted me from Rikers Island immediately after the CD was out. He was halfway through a one-year sentence he received after being arrested carrying a pistol in New York City. He had heard the album's beginning, "I'm Not a Star," on Hot 97 and told me it spoke to him. He wanted to write a song like that when he got out. I had a record ready for him when he arrived. The song became known as "John."

Another thing I learned from that phone call was that Wayne was not receiving the help he deserved during his time of need. Given how many records Wayne had sold for Cash Money Records over the previous decade, I thought it was disgraceful. After the success of Teflon Don, I focused on expanding my label, and that conversation was one of the things that made me consider the type of CEO I wanted to be.

The first musician I wanted to sign with Maybach Music Group was Wiz Khalifa. Spiff had introduced me to Wiz, and I had persuaded him and Curren$y to collaborate on the remix to "Super High." I had the opportunity to meet Wiz properly after flying him and Curren$y to Atlanta to film a video for the song.

Wiz was not only making great music, but he was also more savvy than his stoner attitude suggested. Wiz was ahead of the game when it came to leveraging the internet and social media to establish a fan base, and he had a grassroots movement to support him. His Kush & OJ mixtape was a global trending topic on Twitter for days after its publication. That was an impressive feat for a mixtape with no major label backing. Meanwhile, I'd only learned about Twitter a few months before, when in Hawaii.

I felt Wiz was on his way to becoming a superstar. So I was frustrated that I didn't have the resources to make a deal with him. I didn't have the vast pockets to compete with Atlantic Records, where he eventually signed. That was disheartening, especially since I had declared my desire to sign him on an episode of MTV's RapFix. I attempted to speak it into being, but it did not work. But I didn't let that disappointment deter me. I utilised it for motivation.

I still owed Def Jam a few solo records, but I wanted to find a new home for MMG. Things hadn't been the same there since Shakir died. I'd gotten a taste of having my own imprint, but Maybach's one release—a group album with Triple C's, Custom Cars & Cycles—didn't fare well, and the other artists I'd tried to bring to the label had received little backing from the staff.

Once again, I became the subject of a bidding war. Jimmy Iovine and Puff wanted me to bring Maybach to Interscope and Bad Boy. There was interest from Roc Nation. Khaled had recently signed with Cash Money, and he and Birdman were trying to get me to come.

In the end, Warner Bros. Records won the MMG sweepstakes. In early 2011, I received a call from Dallas Martin. Dallas had been an intern for Shakir when I first signed with Def Jam in 2006. I used to see him at Hitco Studios in Atlanta, where I worked on Port of Miami and Trilla. Shakir would keep him in there listening to demos from sunrise to sunset. Dallas had no influence on my music at the time, but I could sense his enthusiasm.

Dallas was let go when Shakir died, so I was relieved to see him back on his feet. Joie Manda, Warner Bros.' head of urban music, hired him as vice president of A&R. Joie and Dallas wanted to pitch me on taking MMG to Warner Bros, so I invited them to meet me in Toronto, where I had a gig coming up that weekend. That was the weekend Drake lent me his Maybach so Spiff and I could film the video for "Devil in a New Dress."

Dallas' ear had been honed and fine-tuned by Shakir Stewart, the sharpest A&R I'd ever dealt with. He understood the components of a successful record, and he was someone I could rely on to work with any musicians I signed on a daily basis. Then there was Joie. Joie had a great track record during his time at Asylum, where he negotiated a joint venture with Swishahouse, the Houston label responsible for the development of Mike Jones, Paul Wall, and Chamillionaire. That collaboration prepared the groundwork for the Houston Rap conquest in the mid-2000s. And I was informed I'd have the full support of Warner's two top executives, Lyor Cohen and Todd Moscowitz, who wanted to co-manage me with Pucci.

We finalised the agreement over the NBA All-Star Weekend in Los Angeles. Right instantly, I announced my first two signings. I had been scouting for talent throughout the summer.

I first encountered Wale in King of Diamonds. Wale, from what little I knew of him at the time, was a backpack rapper. A true lyricist and unfiltered emcee. So I was astonished to see him in a strip club, and even more surprised to hear his music playing there. He made a tune called "No Hands" featuring Waka Flocka Flame and Roscoe Dash that was causing havoc.

"No Hands" was a hit tune, however it did not really portray Wale as an artist. Wale had depth. He could produce a strip club hymn, but he also wrote songs that spoke to women on a deeper level. He was the blog's poster boy, but he also garnered support from HBCUs and his birthplace of Washington, DC. His music reflected his Nigerian ancestry and included elements of Go-Go and spoken word poetry.

However, Wale's potential had not been fully realised. His popularity on the blogs landed him a deal with Interscope, however he was later released from the company. His debut album, Attention Deficit, was a disaster. But I wasn't bothered with the numbers he'd posted or the debate surrounding his career. Wale caught my attention because of his talent. I told him I was working on straightening out MMG's label situation and that if he could be patient, I'd bring him on board.

A few months later, I was in Philadelphia for a press tour ahead of the publication of Teflon Don. When I arrived, I canvassed my new Twitter followers—I had worked it out after my trip to Hawaii—to see who artists from the city my fans wanted me to collaborate with. The overwhelming answer was Meek Mill. The next day, I did a radio interview at Power 99, and DJ Cosmic Kev invited Meek to visit the station so we could meet.

Meek arrived at the station sporting a black Burberry polo and a rucksack. He was a tall, skinny kid with nappy cornrows, and I assumed that designer polo was the nicest shirt he had. He was getting every last fit out of it—you know how polo collars curl up when they wear out?

Meek was twenty-three years old, but he had been combat rapping on Philadelphia street corners since he was fourteen. T.I. was impressed by his Flamers mixtapes and signed him to Grand Hustle Records in 2008. However, because of their legal issues—Meek had to do six months on gun and drug charges, and T.I. He landed his own federal lawsuit, and the bargain never materialised. So Meek was a free agent.

Meek had a song called "Rosé Red" that was getting a lot of hype, and he asked me to join the remix. I was charging close to six figures for a verse at the time, but I assured him I'd do it on my own strength. I had a hunch about Meek. He possessed the grit and ferocity of the great rappers who emerged from the city of brotherly love before him—niggas such as Beanie Sigel and Freeway—but his music was more than punchlines and double entendre. Meek had a heart. He reminded me of Tupac. The kid was on his way somewhere. Before we parted ways, Meek asked if there was anyone in my camp he could remain in touch with. I gave him my personal phone number, and we stayed in touch from then on.

Months later, when I was about to finalise my deal with Warner Bros., I had my sister fly Meek down to Miami so we could discuss his future. Renee called the next morning, just after I received word that Meek had arrived and was on his way to the house. She sounded flustered.

"Will, I'm sorry, I messed up," she said. "I booked Meek's flight in your name but accidentally did it backwards. "I must be losing my mind."

"He's on his way over to the house though."

That's when we discovered Meek's government name was Robert Williams. I regarded it as a sign. This was a perfect match. When Meek arrived at my place, I showed him $10 million in cash in a duffel bag and informed him that this is what we would start working on if he signed with MMG. He regarded that as a sign as well. We signed the paperwork that day.

Benihana for lunch and then shop. Spiff and I are toy collectors, and one day we discovered a dope-ass toy store and bought insane crap.

Playtime ended at 3:00 p.m. Everyone would then rejoin in the studio. The next twelve hours were all business.

Kanye's creative process was rather crazy. He's a genuine theory. Kanye would be working with me on "Live Fast, Die Young" one minute, then go to check on Nicki's verse on "Monster" in the next room.

Nicki Minaj gained my admiration as a poet that day. I knew she was Lil Wayne's protégé and had a big personality, but when I saw her sit down and craft her verse for "Monster" from scratch, I was astounded. The girl was a celebrity, and she was kicking things off on this record. I persuaded Kanye to let me write a short four-bar bridge that we could insert between the song's beginning and Kanye's hook.

The next thing I knew, I was in a closet with this nice bearded white brother, preparing to record. I'd seen him operating out of a small room in the back. He has been there since I arrived. I assumed he was a stand-in for Mike Dean, Kanye's main engineer who hadn't yet arrived in Hawaii, but he was actually the voice behind the distorted vocals on the song's start. We ended up smoking a lot of joints and kicking the shit as I wrote my little verse.

This hippy motherfucker turned out to be Justin Vernon from the band Bon Iver. But I didn't find out till later. During our time working together, I had no idea who he was and didn't think to ask. I had no doubt that everyone Kanye had flown down here had a valid purpose.

My most significant contribution to My Beautiful Dark Twisted Fantasy came several months following my vacation to Hawaii. Kanye had to turn in his album the following day. But he wanted to get me into "Devil in a New Dress."

I had already recorded a stanza of "Devil in a New Dress" in Hawaii. It was a truly soulful joint, based around an old Smokey Robinson. Kanye previously released the song as part of his weekly G.O.O.D. Friday's series. Except he didn't keep my verse on there. But when I

Then there came Pill, an Atlanta rapper. Warner Bros. had signed Pill a year previously when he gained popularity with a song called "Trap Goin' Ham." He'd been cosigned by Andre 3000 and made XXL magazine's Freshman List, but there appeared to be no progress toward releasing a first album. The label didn't know what to do with him, so I agreed to bring him on board and see what progress he could make under the MMG banner.

I figured it would take a minute to get MMG off the ground and running. But everyone came out of the gates swinging. Meek quickly established himself as one of the game's most talked-about prospects with a one-two punch of singles, "Tupac Back" and "Ima Boss." Wale was proving himself worthy of a second chance at greatness. His showcase effort on Self Made, a song called "That Way" featuring Jeremih and myself, took off as he began to build momentum for his upcoming solo album Ambition.

The accomplishment that we were witnessing inspired me. That spring, I signed two new artists: an emcee from Ohio named Stalley and singer Teedra Moses. I wasn't finished. I signed a young brother from Chicago named Rockie Fresh. I wanted to sign a West Coast artist, so I approached Nipsey Hussle and Dom Kennedy. I wanted to plant the MMG flag in New York, so I attempted to sign French Montana. Those ones didn't work out for various reasons, but I developed ties with all of them and tried to assist them in any way I could nonetheless. Puff had offered a deal to French that I couldn't match, but French still wanted me to executive produce his debut album. MMG was something artists wanted to be a part of, even if it never became official on paper. I really enjoyed that.

My progress was halted that fall when I boarded a Delta trip in Fort Lauderdale. I was on my way to Memphis, where I was due to play at the University of Memphis' "Midnight Madness" event. I was with my on-and-off girlfriend Shateria, Pucci, Sam Sneak, Toie, and Will.

I fell asleep as soon as I took my seat. I'd been working hard, and my schedule was not about to calm down any time soon. At least I had this two-hour flight to get some slumber.

When I opened my eyes, my entire squad surrounded me. Shateria was crying, and everyone else seemed shaken up.

"They're turning the plane around," Pucci explained. "Are they saying you had a seizure?""

I had no memory of what had just happened. My shoulder hurt, but otherwise I felt OK. I saw no need to miss my gig that night. But the flight crew didn't hear it. They asked me to leave the plane.

"Okay, we'll get to the bag later," I said Pucci. "I just performed the Electric Slide!"

Nobody found my joke as amusing as I did. It turns out that having a seizure scares the individuals who observe it more than the person experiencing it.

As soon as we got off the plane, I had my sister call my jet plug and arrange for a private trip to Memphis. An hour later, we were again in the air. After 15 minutes, I experienced another seizure.

When I awoke after the second seizure, I was in a dreamy condition. It wasn't like when I awoke from the first one and everything was fine. I felt sleepy, and my vision was fuzzy. I had no idea where I was or how I had gotten there. I certainly wasn't on a jet. Then I spotted a gun. I assumed I must be in the afterlife.

Damn, someone got me.

As my eyesight returned to focus, I noticed that the revolver I'd seen was holstered on the hip of a police officer standing by my bedside. I was not in heaven. I was at the hospital.

"Where am I?""

"This is UAB Hospital in Birmingham, Alabama," he told me. "I got your back, Boss."

I was not waking up from a seizure. I had just awoken from surgery, and my fuzzy hallucination was due to anaesthetic. During my first seizure, I dislocated my shoulder and tore my labrum. When I boarded the private flight, my shoulder felt really bad. After the orthopaedic surgeon described the details of my shoulder operation, a neurologist entered the room.

The physicians placed electrodes on my head and did an EEG test. There were no abnormalities in my brain activity that suggested I had epilepsy. They ran an MRI and a CT scan, and the results were identical. The neurologist initially did not have a diagnosis for me, but after learning more about my lifestyle, he had a few suggestions.

The doctor was concerned about how little sleep I was receiving. I rarely slept longer than a couple of hours at a time. I might blame it on my schedule, but it was actually due to my restlessness. Even if I went to bed at a respectable hour, I would always lie awake for hours. My thoughts would wander and wouldn't stop. It has been like this for years.

My diet and several vices didn't help either. I did not have the healthiest habits. The doctor was concerned about the amount of marijuana I smoked, but he did not believe it had caused the seizures. He suspected the Tuss may have played a role.

I first started drinking Tussionex a few years ago, during the correctional officer scandal and my conflict with 50 Cent. In retrospect, I believe I picked up the habit to deal with the stress I was experiencing at the time.

Tussionex is a prescription cough syrup. It is prescribed to patients with chronic bronchitis and emphysema. The principal element is hydrocodone, which is similar to codeine. They are both opioids. They slow down your central nervous system. But hydrocodone does so in a more potent manner. Many rappers, including myself at the time, drank codeine and promethazine cough medicine, but few drank Tuss. The lean is purple. You combine it with Sprite. The tuss is yellow. You drank it straight. It's too potent to drink socially, so it wasn't some cool rapper thing. I never announced how I used the cameras. It was something I basically did on my own.

"I'm going to prescribe you some anti-seizure medication but you need to start taking better care of yourself," the medical professional replied. "Get more sleep and cut it out with that stuff you're putting in your body."

I am driven by opposition. Having an opponent across from me has contributed significantly to my success. Sometimes these antagonists are real, like in the case of 50 Cent. Sometimes they are figments of my imagination, like when I thought Ted Lucas and DJ Khaled were holding me back. In any case, the war-mode attitude brings out the best in me. It is what motivates me to keep going when I have every reason in the world to give up. But this time, the opponent was myself. My body and brain had betrayed me. I couldn't make sense of it.

At that point, my mother burst into the room and gave me the largest hug of my life. She started crying, then she started praying. I don't have a lot of dread, but as I hung on to my mother that day, I had never felt more terrified.

Khaled went to the hospital to get me. I didn't even ask him to. As soon as he heard what had happened, he began blowing up Renee's and Pucci's phones to find out where I was. He arrived as soon as he found out.

Khaled is really frightened of flying. I believe he has now overcome that anxiety, but I know he hadn't when this happened because he had recently spent $500,000 on a new tour van. When he arrived at the hospital, he informed me that it was completely at my discretion. I believe Khaled was more concerned about me flying than I was.

"Rozay, I'm telling you, I'll take you wherever you want," stated the man. "But please, do not get back on one of those aeroplanes."

Khaled drove me to my mother's house in Memphis, where I spent the following two weeks on bed rest. It was the longest time I'd taken off since before "Hustlin'." I spent it reading Scripture, enjoying the companionship of my children, and cooking with my mother. Khaled and his wife, Nicole, were with me the entire time. Khaled was still working at 99 Jamz, but he recorded all of his radio spots on the tour bus's mini-studio, allowing him to be with me. That's the type of friend DJ Khaled is.

After taking some time off to heal from surgery and seizures, I felt ready to return to my music. I had an album's worth of material prepared to go. But, before I could release anything, I needed to meet with Def Jam.

My connection with the label had increasingly worsened since L.A. Reid departed to become the chairman and CEO of Epic Records. He was the last of the original trio to sign me in 2006. I wasn't too concerned about L.A., Jay, or Shakir's absence. I no longer required the same level of hands-on instruction that I had when I was first starting out. I have my own in-house team now. What I needed from Def Jam was money. I had outgrown the terms of my initial contract, and we needed to modify my deal to reflect that.

Khaled was my final point of contact at the label. Always a peacemaker, he persuaded Barry Weiss, Def Jam's new CEO, and his team to go down to Miami so we could try to reach an arrangement. He scheduled a lunch meeting at Prime One Twelve. I intentionally arrived an hour late and then began to cuss out everyone present. These folks were not treating me as a top priority, and they needed to comprehend the gravity of their mistake.

Khaled started kicking me beneath the table. Sweat beads collected on his forehead.

"Ross, could you please cool out!"He whispered.

"Oh, by the way... I don't like how you've treated Khaled, either!"

Then I rose up and walked away, leaving Khaled to clean up the mess I had just created.

"You've got a really funny way of expressing love, you know?"He told me later.

If the label decided to play hardball, I was just going to release this music as a mixtape and tour behind it. That would only strengthen my position when I returned to the bargaining table with Def Jam.

The label conflict prompted the publication of Rich Forever, a mixtape that was supposed to be my fifth album. Everyone told me I couldn't just release these records with Nas, Drake, and John Legend for free. It was the same tale Puff told me about "MC Hammer" and "B.M.F."

I knew I would miss out on some short-term record sales, but in the long run, this would only help my stock. My motto has always been, "If it's not a long-term play, it's just small talk." When I released Rich Forever at the beginning of 2012, my gamble on myself paid off handsomely. It made no difference what format the release was. The music spoke for itself.

Rich Forever was a showcase for my second characteristic sound. My first was what I refer to as the "Maybach sound." Luxurious, soulful tracks like "Maybach Music" and "Cigar Music" transport listeners into a different tax bracket. Rich Forever was all about street records. It was a sound I had developed with Lex Luger on songs like "B.M.F." and "MC Hammer" and proceeded to improve on Self Made Vol. 1. Rich Forever was my way of polishing it.

Then I went on a fourteen-date European tour and earned all of the money I'd asked Def Jam for myself. At that moment, the label agreed to meet my expectations. They recognized that the longer they let this issue play out, the more it would cost them. After Def Jam cut the check, I began working on God Forgives, I Don't.

I had gone big with each of my albums, but this was going to be the largest. I wanted this record to be like a blockbuster picture. I was influenced by the works of Mario Puzzo, Quentin Tarantino, and Martin Scorsese. I wanted the track list for God Forgives, I Don't to resemble Scorsese's cast for The Departed, when he managed to cast Jack Nicholson, Leo DiCaprio, Matt Damon, Mark Wahlberg, and Alec Baldwin all in the same film. This would be epic in that sense.

Dr. Dre has been my idol since I first started making music. As a child, my record library was packed with Ruthless Records albums, and the prospect of one day working in the studio with Dre had been a lifetime ambition. When I was in Hawaii working with Kanye on My Beautiful Dark Twisted Fantasy, those studio sessions reminded me of Dre's The Chronic. This genius is putting together a masterpiece from all these varied contributions.

But out of respect for Dre, I never pursued our collaboration. I knew that would put him in an awkward situation, with 50 Cent tied to Aftermath. I didn't want to cause problems for one of my main influences, so I let that goal go. But I did not let it die.

I ended up connecting with The D.O.C., who co-wrote The Chronic with Dre, and we got into a discussion about Dre's role in hip-hop history. To my amazement, D.O.C. informed me that the regard was mutual. A few days later, he put me on the phone with Dre, who said he'd be in Miami in a few weeks and suggested we lock in. Of course, I cleared my schedule.

Dre travelled to Miami with gifts. Dre got this beat from an A&R at Aftermath. Jake One produced it, and it sampled Crowns of Glory's gospel classic "I'm So Grateful". It reminded me of a recent record I did with Drake called "Lord Knows." I wrote lyrics for both of us, and we finished the song the first day at Circle House Studios. We didn't complete it, though. There was only one thing remaining to do to expand this relationship beyond its current scope. Of course, I had to put Jay-Z on there. I had originally planned to have Jay-Z work on a different song for God Forgives, I Don't, but that could wait. He had to be on this. That's how "3 Kings" was conceived.

If I was going to get Dre and Hov on a record, I felt I may as well take my chance and see what other collaborations I could tick off my bucket list. I had obtained a beat from J.U.S.T.I.C.E League that sounded like vintage Outkast. I was able to connect with the mysterious Andre 3000 over Skype when he was filming a Jimi Hendrix biography in Europe.

I informed Andre that fourteen years ago, I opened for Outkast at Studio 183 in Carol City. I wasn't even known as Teflon da Don back then. I was still rapping as Willow. Outkast was in town for a pre-release celebration for their third album, Aquemini. A week before the performance, the promoter held a competition in which participants could come up to Studio 183 and perform a song. Whoever has the greatest idea got to open for Outkast. It ended up being me.

Opening for Outkast is always an unforgettable experience, but this one was very remarkable for another reason. The date was Friday, September 11, 1998. It was the day the feds apprehended Jabbar. That's why I wasn't up in Jacksonville. I'd returned to Miami to open for Outkast.

This was the first time Andre 3000 and I had spoken, so I wasn't going to go into the whole tale. I just told him I used to open up for him and Big Boi, and it was an honour for us to be talking about recording music now. Andre enjoyed the beat and was eager to get involved, but as an innovator, making a "vintage Outkast" single was insufficient. We began to discuss breaking the mould of hip-hop's traditional sixteen-bar verse. Sixteen wasn't enough, either. This discussion ended in the eight-minute epic "Sixteen," in which Andre gave a famous verse and an electric guitar solo at the conclusion. Three stacks went full Jimi on that girl.

Then I received further features from Drake, Usher, and Ne-Yo. I received beats from Pharrell. These things are expensive, so I used up all of my recording budget from Def Jam before requesting more. The uncredited feature from Los Angeles. Reid on "Maybach Music IV" did not cost me a thing, however. Certain things in life are priceless. That was a little wink at the label, similar to the one I gave Atlantic Records on "Hustlin'" back in 2005.

God Forgives, I did not achieve the highest figures in my profession. For the fourth time, my record debuted at number one on the Billboard charts, and for the first time, I surpassed the 200,000 mark with 218,000 first-week sales. A month later, it was declared Gold. I imagined Scorsese winning Best Picture at the Academy Awards.

Chapter 16

My thirty-sixth year has been full of blessings. It was only fitting that I celebrate my thirty-seventh birthday in style. We went all out that night. In fact, we went all out that weekend. After taking over Club Compound in Atlanta on Saturday, I flew home on Sunday to celebrate my birthday at LIV. I was wearing an all-white suit with a red button-up underneath and velvet Versace Medusa slippers on my feet. And I was wearing a huge gold Cuban link around my neck. I resembled Tony Montana when he went to meet Sosa in Cochabamba. I didn't realise I'd be living like Scarface in more ways than one that night.

We converted LIV into The Babylon. Everyone was in the club that night. Puff was there. French was present. Fabolous. Ludacris. Christina Milian and Scott Storch. The entire MMG family was there. All of my Carol City niggas from day one were present. Shateria stood at my side in a black minidress and thigh-high boots. We were opening bottles of Luc Belaire. We were smoking large blunts. We were having a birthday cake. It was simply one of those evenings.

I exited the club just after 4:00 a.m. Shateria and I climbed into a silver Rolls-Royce Phantom. Black and one of my security officers were following me in the vehicle. As I crossed the bridge connecting Miami Beach and the Miami I knew, I had a moment of reflection. Many niggas in my hometown never visit the beach. But I did. And I'd gotten far further than the Fontainebleau.

I got on Interstate 95 and drove home. As I approached the Fort Lauderdale exit, I contacted Black and told him I'd take it from there. I was on my way to my house in the Seven Isles. Everyone else was staying in the studio house in Davie. They didn't need to drive an extra hour at 5 a.m. to escort me the rest of the way home. At least I assumed they didn't.

I came to a stop at a red light on the corner of Las Olas Boulevard and 15th Avenue, five minutes away from my residence. Shateria and I were having a heated disagreement about a girl she had seen me chatting to in the club when I heard the bullets.

Pop, pop, pop, pop!

"911, what is your emergency?"

"I just heard several gunshots and saw a car speed by. And my server just departed on her bike to go somewhere—Oh my God, they're turning around and coming back! I am hanging up! I am hanging up! Bye!"

"Okay, ma'am, how many shots did you hear?"

"I do not know! I don't know. But they are coming back! "I am hiding!"

Witnesses later told police that four males pulled up in a maroon BMW and opened fire. But I did not see the gunmen. I didn't see the car, either. I only heard the gunshots. I knew they were made of sticks based on the sound they made. They were far too loud and rapid to have come from a handgun.

I accelerated and peeled off. I went into 15th Avenue from Las Olas, but I overshot. I was driving intoxicated, high, and barefooted. My father constantly taught me never to drive barefoot.

I leaned to my right to cover Shateria, but before I could look up and straighten up the wheel, I lost control of my car and collided into the apartment building behind The Floridian cafe. The airbags detonated in our faces.

When I tried to open my door, I couldn't. It was crowded. I looked at Shateria.

"Run!"

Shateria exited the vehicle on the passenger side and ran behind the building. I finally opened my door and stepped outside to follow her. Then I heard the squeal of a car turning around on Las Olas. They were coming back around.

Please tell me Shateria did not simply run behind the house we collided into. That is the first place they will look. Any house but that one.

I dashed back to the car and retrieved my Cuban link. These niggas weren't going away with my chain. That chunk weighed four kilograms of pure gold. It cost me $160,000. Then I grabbed my chrome Smith & Wesson 9mm, which had fallen between the seats during the crash. I wasn't going to leave Shateria, but I also wasn't going to be caught unarmed when these shooters discovered us.

I ran behind the building but could not find Shateria. It was 5 a.m., so I couldn't see anything. The backyard was fenced in, so I knew she had to be here. There was only one entrance and one exit. I drew my pistol from my waistband and prepared for a standoff. A full clip contained fifteen bullets, but I wasn't sure how many were loaded at the time. Hopefully, we'll have enough to get out of there.

By God's grace, I would not need any bullets. After doing a U-turn on Las Olas, the gunmen took off north on 16th Avenue.

I eventually discovered Shateria huddled up in a ball under the back porch. She was shaking so fiercely that I believed she had been hit. She hadn't, but she was close to having a panic attack. Shateria was hyperventilating when I discovered her. When I returned, she heard my footsteps but couldn't see me from underneath the porch. So she just sat there silently.

Police came a few minutes later and taped off the murder scene. Eighteen gunshot shells were discovered dispersed over the streets and in two stores. But they had not hit the automobile. Were they attempting to murder me and failing miserably, or were they simply conveying a message?

The cops took Shateria and me inside the diner to record our statements. They started asking a lot of police-ass questions.

"Do you have any idea who did this?"

"I don't."

"Okay, we know who you are... Do you suppose this had anything to do with the Carol City Cartel?"

"Triple C's is a music group."

"Right... What about the Gangster's disciples? Is it true that you've been having issues with them?

"Who?"

"Didn't you have to cancel some shows recently?"

"I have no idea what you're talking about."

"What about 50 Cent?"

"The donkey?"

"Excuse me?"

"Detectives, with all due respect, my lawyer can assist you with the remainder of your questions. It has been a long night. "I need to rest."

"Look, we're just trying to get to the bottom of what happened."

"Me, too. "Good luck with that."

Black Bo and Pucci had arrived by then, and he wanted to hear what had transpired. I told him to have my sister book rooms for everyone at the St. Regis. This had occurred so near to the house that I knew Shateria would be unable to sleep there.

My brand-new Phantom was now sitting on the back of a flatbed tow truck. The entire front was caved in. So Shateria and I hired a driver to take us to Bal Harbour. The sun had risen by then, and I was fatigued. Staying up all night drinking and smoking was quite normal for me, but surviving a drive-by shooting was not. I had escaped the crisis on adrenaline, but now I was fading quickly.

We'd arrive at the hotel soon. There we would get to the bottom of everything. My mom and Renee were on their way to Miami. My lawyer was, too. We could all have a debrief at the hotel. In the meantime, I needed a little nap.

When I opened my eyes, I noticed Shateria's horrified expression. She was hilarious. Something had just happened. I peered out the window and noticed that we were still in Fort Lauderdale. I hadn't been sleeping for more than five minutes. But I had overlooked something.

"Take us to the hospital!" she exclaimed. "Please! "He is having a seizure!"

From the outside, 2012 had been a year of complete dominance. I'd made the cover of The Source's "Man of the Year" issue for the second year in a row. I then topped MTV's Hottest MCs list. God Forgives, I Don't was the biggest album of my career. Meek and Wale were both thriving at MMG.

However, the year had not gone as well as it appeared. The drive-by shooting on my birthday was the culmination of everything that had been simmering below the surface.

When I first released "B.M.F.," a group of niggas claiming to be Gangster's Disciples were upset because I mentioned Larry Hoover, the Chicago gang's incarcerated leader. I was obviously praising Hoover in the song, so their intentions sounded questionable from the start, but out of respect for the OG, I met with Larry Hoover Jr. when in Chicago to promote the release of Teflon Don. He told me that his old man had no issues with me. And that was pretty much it.

The problem, which had never been anything to begin with, went dormant for two years until I released The Black Bar Mitzvah mixtape. This group of so-called GDs was now accusing me of using the gang's six-pointed insignia without permission and issuing threats. The mixtape cover clearly depicted a Star of David rather than the GD sign. At that point, I understood the issue. This was an extortion attempt, and unfortunately for the niggas, no checks were cut.

The week before The Black Bar Mitzvah's release, I had a confrontation with another individual who had a problem with "B.M.F.," Young Jeezy. Jeezy had run with Big Meech and BMF in their prime, and for some reason, he felt a certain way about me paying tribute to his OG. Jeezy and I had collaborated on various albums throughout the years—he was on the "Hustlin'" remix back in '06—but since "B.M.F.", he'd been slick dissing and sending small subliminal bullets my way. Of course, I repaid him in kind.

So when I saw Jeezy backstage at the 2012 BET Hip-Hop Awards in Atlanta, I contacted him to discuss any concerns that needed to be resolved. To me, the whole affair seemed minor, so I was prepared to crush any beef. But I was also prepared for any smoke if Jeezy chose to go that route. Unfortunately, we were unable to reach an arrangement. Our teams collided and were swiftly separated by cops.

Gunplay should not have attended the BET Hip-Hop Awards in the first place. He was on the run for armed robbery and assault with a lethal weapon following an incident at his accountant's office earlier that year.

When the scenario with Jeezy escalated, there was no gunplay, but he became aware of a ruckus. When he started bouncing around, trying to figure out what had happened, no one gave him a straight explanation. Everyone knew better than to say something that would ruffle Gunplay up. People were trying to de-escalate the situation.

But Gunplay Murdoch isn't the type of person who has to know every detail of a situation before going in headfirst. He assumed that if MMG had just gotten into it with some niggas, it must have been 50 and G-Unit. So, when Gunplay saw 50 and his secret service security team in the parking lot, he opted to square off against all eight of them. A struggle erupted, and Gunplay lost his chain and was stung by a thousand bees. Security pepper-sprayed him, and he scrambled into 2 Chainz's trailer before getting someone to get him the heck out.

Don't even question why Gunplay was out alone. You've got to ask that insane motherfucker why he acts like that. That's just gunplay.

All of this is to imply that I'd been having a lot of troubles with niggas. So when the cops inquired who fired up my Phantom, I said I had no idea who it could be.

I am not in the business of launching investigations, and I will never engage in one. But I will admit that it was not the first time niggas attempted to kill me that year. There was another occurrence. One that didn't make the news. This was similar to what happened on my birthday. The same situation. The same sound of a helicopter ringing off. Except that I wasn't with Shateria in my Phantom. I was in a Maybach. It did not pass by my residence in Seven Isles. It happened somewhere else. And we didn't wreck the car that time. I got out and started blowing it. I have talked too much. Let's leave it there.

Psalm 27 1:4 is my favourite Bible verse. After seeing what I've seen, I've regarded it as a picture of a young nigga overcoming death. These verses have helped me get through difficult times.

Who am I to fear when the Lord is my light and salvation? Who am I to be scared of while the Lord is my stronghold?

When the wicked come against me to eat me, my enemies and foes will stumble and fall.

Even if an army besieges me, my heart will not be afraid; if a battle breaks out against me, I will remain confident.

I only beg the Lord for one thing: that I may live in the Lord's house for the rest of my life, gazing on his splendour and seeking him in his temple.

Like I previously stated, I have no idea who attempted to take my life. But what if I had to bet? I bet it had nothing to do with the stupid industry nonsense you read about on blogs. I bet it was about something else. And I bet every gunner on the hit squad is dead as a doornail.

Chapter 17

Homes have always been a source of inspiration to me. My parents were both interested in real estate, and they taught my sister and me the value of ownership and equity. They did not believe in investing their savings in the stock market. They wanted to be able to handle their money. My father used to remind me that a man's job isn't complete unless he can provide a home for his family.

When Jabbar and I used to commute to Atlanta, I would always have him drive me past the Holyfield estate before we headed home. 794 Evander Holyfield Highway, Fayetteville, Georgia. We'd pull over to the side of the road, smoke a half-joint, and take everything in.

Lord, have mercy.

Villa Vittoriosa. "The Victory." I originally saw the property on an episode of ESPN Sportscenter. The former heavyweight champion had just had it built, and it was a sight to see. A 45,000-square-foot home spread across 105 acres.

The apartment has everything. Twelve bedrooms. Twenty-one restrooms. A dining area that could accommodate one hundred guests. A movie theatre. A bowling alley. An indoor basketball court. A tennis court. A softball field. A horse barn with seven stalls. Behind the house sat the United States' largest residential swimming pool. Of course, it had an indoor pool.

In 2006, just after the Port of Miami went gold, I purchased my first million-dollar home a mile from the estate. So I'd always bike by and admire the Holyfield mansion, just like I did back in 1996. Then one day, in the fall of 2013, I noticed a For Sale sign on the fence. I quickly dialled the number on the listing.

Evander Holyfield's property had gone into foreclosure and was now held by JPMorgan Chase & Co. It was another tragic story in boxing history about previous greats going bankrupt. Joe Louis died impoverished and addicted to narcotics. Leon Spinks went from beating Muhammad Ali in the Las Vegas Hilton to scrubbing restrooms at a YMCA in Nebraska. Mike Tyson made $300 million during his career and went bankrupt. And Holyfield struggled to pay child support for his twelve children and six baby mothers.

Everyone warned me about the costs of running a company like this. They said the upkeep cost more than a million dollars every year. Christmas lights alone incurred a $17,000 electric bill. But I needed to have this place. It seemed like my destiny.

I'd sell my Seven Isles home if it came to it. I spent $5,000,000 for a three-story mansion that included eight bedrooms, a movie theatre, an arcade, and a gym. It was right on the sea, and I had a 90-foot yacht called Rich Forever drifting out back. That place was amazing. But it was not the Holyfield house.

This house was a symbol of possibilities. The location I used to fantasise about when I had nothing could now be mine. And it would not be just mine. This would be something that my entire family could appreciate and take pride in. Somewhere my children could meet all of their friends and cousins and have a great time.

I was still undecided about acquiring the property until I had the opportunity to meet with Honourable Minister Louis Farrakhan in November. Farrakhan brought me to his farm in Michigan, where he discussed the value of owning land and how, previous to integration, black people owned a lot of it. He discussed how, in order to share toilets with white people and support their companies, we ignored and lost our own.

From the outside, purchasing the Holyfield house seems reckless. But at $5.8 million, it was a fantastic steal. I'm not sure how much Holyfield spent on the estate, but he was suddenly in the hole for $14 million. When the bank purchased the property, they initially listed it for $8.2 million. I was going to make a good profit if I sold the Seven Isles crib. More than enough to justify purchasing this one.

I knew I wouldn't have the same destiny as Holyfield. The truth was that I had managed my money wisely. I'm no genius, but I can make genius moves. One of my wisest decisions was to delegate responsibility for my non-music investments to my mother and sister. Both of them had always been involved in managing my finances behind the scenes, but when Renee resigned her day job and began working for me full-time, the money began to pile up.

Any company I partnered with had to be one that I personally admired. It had to be something I wanted to promote in my music and feel good about in all I did. Wingstop fit the bill. I had been a longtime fan of their lemon pepper wings (all flats, of course), and I enjoyed how they differed from their competition. At Hooters, your money goes toward flat-screen televisions and waitresses' boob jobs. At Wingstop, you pay for your wings. I opened my first franchise in Memphis in 2011. Three years later, I had nine outlets and intend to treble that number in the next few years.

Renee and I planned to buy the Checkers in Carol City next. When I was thirteen years old and working at the car wash, there was a Checkers across the street. There was a McDonald's right next to the car wash, but a Big Buford was somewhat cheaper than a Big Mac. I was only paid $30 per day plus tips, so the minor price difference made a significant difference to me. It was worth walking across the street. When I was in high school, Checkers was where my football team went to celebrate after beating another school's ass. This was another local business that I had a personal relationship with and was excited to support.

Then I received my ownership part in Luc Belaire. Brett Berish, the founder and CEO of Sovereign Brands, owned and operated Luc Belaire, a French sparkling rosé brand. Sovereign Brands was the parent business of Armand de Brignac, a $300-per-bottle champagne known as the Ace of Spades. Jay-Z, who had owned a stake in Ace of Spades since its inception in 2006, was ready to buy out Berish and gain full ownership of the company.

I have a lot of respect for Hov for that piece and the whole tale behind it. It began when all rappers popped bottles of Cristal in their music videos. A reporter questioned the company's director how he felt about the hip-hop community's embrace of the brand.

"What can we do?"" he stated. "We can't forbid people from buying it."

Hip-hop had generated millions of dollars in income for this firm, and that was how we were compensated. Jay-Z pulled every bottle of Cris from the shelf at his 40/40 Club and declared a boycott of the brand. Then he went into company with Brett Berish, and Ace of Spades was born. So when the opportunity to collaborate with Brett and participate in his newest initiative, Luc Belaire, arose, I needed no persuasion. And it took off. Today, it is the best-selling French sparkling wine in the United States.

My success in life, whether in music or business, is not the result of me doing one faultless chess move after another. I didn't get where I am because I never accepted defeat. It took ten years for people to accept my music. I wasn't able to sign every musician I wanted to MMG, and not every artist I did sign did well. Not every Wingstop site moved chickens in the way I needed them to. That year, I lost an endorsement deal with Reebok because of a phrase in a song called "U.O.E.N.O." A few years later, I faced similar anger for a comment I made about not signing female rappers to MMG because I would want to sleep with them.

I try not to amuse the Twitter mob or gossip blogs. I learnt from the CO debate that the media is more interested in causing controversy than in telling the truth. It doesn't take much study to discover that I've spent my whole career working with female artists. Or that my mother and sister form the foundation of my kingdom. However, some individuals would rather blow up a single offensive lyric or an off-handed comment in a radio interview and portray me as someone I am not.

Let's keep it real for a second. This is Ricky Rozay. You came to hear some true gangster trash, right? Saying some fucked-up crap comes with the territory. My music portrays a specific type of setting. If you're going to get upset about every offensive phrase, you might want to seek another genre. I can admit to occasionally crossing the line and uttering something terrible, but please refrain from grasping the pearls. At the end of the day, my actions define me. I can stand by them.

Let me go back to what I was saying. I've taken my share of losses. There have been numerous. But I never allowed them to break me. When you pursue a desire, you will undoubtedly face challenges. You're going to muck things up so badly that everyone and their mother will tell you to stop. Success comes from saying "fuck it." I ain't done yet," and then giving it another try. Resilience is what creates success.

As I was closing on the Holyfield House, I was finishing Mastermind. My sixth album's title came from debates regarding Napoleon Hill's Mastermind Principle. Jabbar recommended Hill's book The Law of Success, which he had read while incarcerated. Jabbar has just returned from his second trip to the feds. He had been home for two years after serving his ten-year term in 1998 when he was arrested in another case outside of Arizona. I prayed that this time my homie would be home for good.

I set the stage for Mastermind with my sixth collaboration with Jay-Z, "The Devil Is a Lie." Originally, I wanted to get Hov on another beat, a record produced by Boilda and Vinlyz that's now known as "FuckWithMeYouKnowIGotIt." But when Jay heard the beat, he wanted to keep it for himself. Hov was working on his first solo album in four years, Magna Carta Holy Grail, and he had gifted me with so many timeless verses throughout the years that I had to let him have them. I was overjoyed to finally get a spot on one of his albums. Of course, he returned the favour tenfold in "The Devil Is a Lie."

I had to make a similar move to get "Mafia Music III" onto Mastermind. That was a track I originally wrote for Dr. Dre while he was working on Detox. I created verses for him and myself, and the story was that Dre was going to hire Rihanna to sing the hook. But another story I heard was that Detox will never be released.

Khaled and I both enjoy island music, so we were drawn to this establishment. If Dre wasn't doing anything with it, I needed it for Mastermind. I intended to amplify the beat's dancehall vibes by featuring some authentic Jamaican performers, such as Mavado and Sizzla. Khaled hit Bink!, the beat's producer, who obtained Dr. Dre's permission for me to keep "Mafia Music III."

Puff was the final piece in the Mastermind puzzle. I paid the big homie a visit at his home on Star Island two weeks before the album's release date. I needed him to sign off on "Nobody," which was a remake of "You're Nobody (Til Somebody Kills You)," the foreboding outro to Biggie's final album, Life After Death. The song was conceived during a studio session with French Montana. I wanted to confront the recent attempts on my life, but I couldn't do so directly. I knew too much. I wanted to approach it ambiguously, much as you never knew for sure if Big was talking about Tupac on the record.

I had previously contacted D-Roc, Big's right-hand man who was in the car with him the night he was killed. He gave me his blessings. Now I need two items from Puff. The first step involved sample clearance. I wasn't concerned about that portion. I knew Puff would adore what I did there. The second thing I wasn't sure about. One of Puff's Revolt staffers had handed me a recording of him blacking out on one of his musicians during a session.

"You fuckin' want to walk around with these niggas..." Where the hell is their culture? Where the fuck are their souls? What defines you? These niggas with fucking stupid expressions on their faces... YOU WANT TO WALK WITH THEM OR WITH GOD, NIGGA?! MAKE UP YOUR DAMN MIND!"

Puff is well-known for his famous rants, but this one ranks among the best of all time. I wanted to use it in the song. I promised Puff that I would keep the identity of the person getting it a secret, and he gave me the thumbs up. He understood the audience needed to hear him speak that way.

After listening to Mastermind several times, I asked Puff what he believed was still missing. He told me that all the elements of a classic album were already present. I only needed to create it all in one piece. Mastermind had to feel like everything was recorded in the same booth on the same day. As if I, Hov, Kanye, Lil Wayne, The Weeknd, and everyone else involved had been drinking and smoking in the studio while we were recording. The way albums were produced in the 1990s. There was only one person with the necessary knowledge and experience to get me there. I requested Puff to join me as executive producer and assist me finish the album.

All of my previous albums had been mixed and mastered in a few hours. Puff's process lasted several days. I learned a lot while watching him blend Mastermind. I had always been meticulous about my music, but I would polish it one tune at a time. Puff took a bird's-eye perspective of Mastermind. It wasn't enough for Mike Will Made It's high hats, snares, and kicks to be heavy on "War Ready." They had to be as heavy as the other producers' on the album.

Mastermind released a terrific album that delivered in terms of statistics. Between the shooting on my birthday and being dropped by Reebok, 2013 had been a little difficult, but I felt like things were starting to get better. However, more storms were on the way, and my resilience would soon be tested.

On June 21, 2014, I was set to perform at the Hot 107.5 Summer Jamz festival in Detroit. But when we arrived at the place, the gates were padlocked, and there were a lot of niggas standing around. The show promoter spoke with Pucci, who was in the car ahead of me. After a brief conversation, Pucci called our car and said we were returning to the casino to hang out while the promoter resolved an issue. We departed, and I didn't think much about the incident until we arrived at the casino and noticed the chat on Twitter.

It turned out that Trick Trick, a local rapper, had come to Chene Park with a hundred of his goons to stop me from performing. Trick Trick declared Detroit a "No Fly Zone," which required out-of-towners to check in with him before performing in his hometown. Trick Trick was not well-known for his music, but he had a reputation for doing sucker shit like this. He jumped Trick Daddy back in the day for "stealing his name" and beat him almost to death. As if anyone was even aware who Trick Trick was. Trick Trick must have missed the notice that I did not conduct check-ins. What I didn't understand was why he turned us away if he wanted to have a confrontation. If you are from the bush, you do not keep the lions out. You allowed them in!

When Trick Trick was asked what the problem was, he said it was between him and me, but there was none. I wasn't sure if he was seeking a handout or just some attention, but he wasn't getting it. I didn't feel compelled to shoot my way into a place to perform, but I felt sorry for all the kids who came out to watch me that evening. These were the ones who lost out.

Before I could figure out what this loser was unhappy about, I had a serious problem. Meek was sentenced to three to six months in prison after breaking the terms of his probation. Genece Brinkley, the judge who had been obsessed with him since he heard his case in 2008, alleged that Meek had broken the terms of his probation by not obtaining her permission to fly out of town for a show. That may have been accurate, but the punishment appeared disproportionate.

The timing was bad. Meek's sophomore album, Dreams Worth More Than Money, was slated to be released in September. That was not going to happen now. Wale was still working on his record, and I knew he wouldn't hurry to compensate for Meek's shortcomings. They were not on good terms. A personal feud between Meek and Wale had broken out on social media a few days prior. It was not something serious. Just a disagreement between two passionate artists and brothers. But, of course, the blogs were having a field day with the tale, which did not reflect well on my brand.

One of the reasons I released two albums in eight months was due to the loss of Meek's release date. I'd never published two albums in a single calendar year before, but I thought the team needed to put some numbers on the board in what was shaping up to be a down year.

Hood Billionaire was some hard Geechi crap with a lot of great concepts. Much of the album was influenced by my love of Memphis. I'd spent a lot of time there that summer setting up my new Wingstop sites. I even received a key to the city from Mayor A.C. Wharton for bringing so many jobs to the area. The album's first song, "Elvis Presley Boulevard," was an homage to the cradle of rock and roll, including North Memphis icon Project Pat on it. Other Memphis artists including Yo Gotti and K. Michelle were also on the CD.

The other aspect of Hood Billionaire was my reunion with an old friend. Kenny "Boobie" Williams. Boobie and I had been in contact since he was imprisoned, but this was the first time he authorised me to include him in my music. Boobie called in from USP McCreary in Kentucky, where he is serving a life sentence, and my engineer E-Mix captured the conversation so that we could include snatches of it throughout the album.

There were some great records on Hood Billionaire. The issue was that I didn't go through it with a fine-toothed comb as I usually do. Take "Movin' Bass" as an example. Jay-Z and I collaborated on "Movin' Bass" the same day we recorded

"FuckWithMeYouKnowIGotIt" in New York. Hov performed a hook during the session but did not get to a verse. We only had him mumbling a freestyle over the music before we had to part ways.

The turnaround for Hood Billionaire was so quick that we couldn't thoroughly revisit the song. But I wanted to do something with the record. Hov gave us permission to utilise his hook but not any of his unfinished verses.

The record still sounded good, and I could have gotten away with half a Jay-Z feature if not for Timbaland. Timbaland was at the studio that day and had access to the session's files. He leaked a version of the song with Hov's illegal vocals and put one of his artists on it before my album was even out. It made it appear that this was the original version of the song and mine was a counterfeit. I was so upset with Timberland for doing that thing.

When Hood Billionaire came out, it was clear that it had been rushed. It sold half as many copies as Mastermind. My money was at an all-time high, but that was not what I was concerned about. I just didn't enjoy letting my fans down.

Between label infighting, Meek's arrest, and the first commercial and critical failure of my career, 2014 was not the return to form I had hoped for. And MMG did not appear to be the untouchable empire that I claimed it was. I was out here looking feeble.

Chapter 18

2015 was meant to be a rebuilding year. At first, things looked promising. Wale's album About Nothing debuted at number one. Meek returned home after five months at Curran-Fromhold Correctional Facility. He was finishing up Dreams Worth More Than Money. Even wild-ass Gunplay had a release date set for his long-awaited solo album. The crew was still together. The movement was still ongoing.

I wasn't in a hurry to release another album after releasing Mastermind and Hood Billionaire so close together. At the time, my primary emphasis was on myself. Over the last year, I'd lost about 100 pounds, but there was still work to be done. Since the seizures, I've known I needed to start taking better care of myself. But it wasn't until I discovered CrossFit and put my own twist on it—which I named RossFit—that the pounds began to fall off.

I was eating better, too. I had hired a personal chef, Amaris, and she was making things easy for me. The first thing I did was switch from Coke to water. Then Amaris started giving me a drink after my workouts that tasted so fantastic I assumed it was Hawaiian Punch. It turned out to be beet juice mixed with organic strawberries and a touch of lemonade. Then Amaris lured me into consuming cauliflower. She mixed it up and presented it to me alongside short ribs. I could swear it was mashed potatoes. Who would have guessed Rozay would drink beet juice and eat cauliflower? And if I happen to be in the mood for dessert after dinner at Prime One Twelve, I'll indulge. A boss has no restrictions. Sometimes a boss needs to eat like a boss.

Speaking of Amaris, she was riding shotgun when my troubles began that summer. She had just arrived in Atlanta, and we had planned to visit a nursery and purchase a large number of herb and vegetable plants. We were about to start Rozay Farms and cultivate everything there. Collard green plants. Tomatoes. Cucumbers. Sweet potatoes. I really wanted to find an Asian pear tree. A shout out to all the pears. We had the entire day planned out. However, as soon as we pulled out of the house, we were stopped by the Fayette County Sheriff's Office. As Deputy Sheriff Tommy Grier came out of his vehicle and began walking toward us, I looked over at Amaris and assured her that everything would be fine. She was already praying, clutching her rosary beads.

Grier appeared to be the type of person who enjoyed cutting eye holes in his bedsheets and wearing them over his head when he wasn't in uniform. He said he had pulled me over for having unlawful window tinting. "Too dark," he said. I knew it wasn't about that. I hadn't spoken with the police in Fayette County since I acquired the Holyfield house, and now they were waiting outside my property to inspect the tints on my Mulsanne.

"Is that your house you came out of?"

"It is."

"Why does your car have Florida tags?"

"Because I live in Florida too."

"Well, Mr. Roberts, you'll have to modify those. "You're now in Fayetteville, Georgia." Clearly, this was not an ordinary traffic stop. I was handcuffed and imprisoned in the back of the cruiser after Grier reported smelling marijuana and calling for backup. It was a lie. There was some marijuana in the car—I have people driving my cars and rolling my joints all day long—but he couldn't have smelled a couple of joints sitting in a plastic bag beneath the floorboard. It wasn't as if I was smoking in the car when he pulled us over. We'd just left the house.

But Grier's claim that he smelt cannabis gave him the plausible reason he needed to search my car. He eventually discovered the joints. He also found my Glock. I have an active licence to carry weapons, so there should have been no issue. But the grin on Grier's face told me he was thrilled with his discovery.

Amaris began crying as a female cop came on the scene and handcuffed her. I could see her knees buckle. I don't think Amaris has ever received a parking ticket. That's when I started feeling horrible about Grier. I assured him Amaris had nothing to do with what was in my car, but he didn't care. Even Grier's partner, Deputy Tyler Simpson, believed she should be fired. Simpson was another huge, thick-naked white guy, but he remained cool and respectful the entire time. Grier was the only one that fucked with us. I told him he was a donut-eating fat fuck, that his wife was cheating on him, and that when he found out, he would forgive her because that's the kind of pussy cracker he is. Grier attempted to respond, but lacked the intelligence to match my insults. He was out of his league.

I talked shit to Grier the entire way to Fayette County Jail, and I walked in that bitch screaming at the top of my lungs. I had to create a precedence for how I would be handled here.

"Rozay is inside the motherfucking building!" Which of you fucking pigs are going to grab me some Wingstop?!"

Deputy Simpson took me to the short-term holding cell, where he removed my handcuffs. I repeatedly told him not to.

"Leave them on!" I want Grier to take them off! Grier put them on me. Please have him take those off, too!"

Grier walked out of an office a few minutes later, carrying a stack of binders. He began bragging to his coworkers.

"Seems like I'm all over TMZ! I suppose this guy is a big-time rapper."

Fear Grier pretended he had no idea who resided in Fayetteville's most famous house. This guy was a loser.

After ten hours in central booking, I was charged for a misdemeanour marijuana charge. I was released a few hours later after posting a $2,400 bail bond. I had met and chopped it up with a few actual niggas in there, so on my way out, I also paid their bonds.

Amaris wouldn't be released for another twelve hours. My fingerprints and other information were already in the system because I had previously been arrested. They had nothing on her and needed to ensure she wasn't giving them a bogus alias. Finally, they let her leave. I sent her on vacation to Paris the next week since I felt terrible for putting her through that nightmare. She was traumatised.

I was on my way home, but I knew whatever was going on wasn't over. Two weeks later, I found out.

This is how things went down. Jonathan and Leo were workmen who had previously worked on one of my Miami residences. At the time,

I was working under the supervision of my general contractor, Garabello.

When I bought the Holyfield estate, Garabello moved to Georgia with his entire crew, including Jonathan and Leo. There was a lot of work to do, and it would take some time to get this business up and running. The groundskeeping had been neglected for many years. The house required remodelling. Furnishing all 109 rooms required its own technique.

Among his many tasks, Black Bo was the estate's property manager. He monitored the entire project and provided me with regular updates. Because Garabello did not speak English, Black communicated more with Jonathan, who was bilingual. Jonathan eventually became a mediator between the two.

Long story short, I let Garabello go. But I kept Jonathan. Jonathan vouched for Leo, thus he was let to stay. Because neither of them was from Georgia, I let them stay at the guest home. I was still living in the studio house. The enormous mansion was still a work in progress, and security was a concern. We'd had incidents of people climbing the gates. The community had yet to adjust to the property's new ownership, and it had not been made plain that trespassing would not be permitted. That is why I was still residing at the studio house.

On the morning of June 7, Black went over to the large house to check on things. It was Sunday. Nine out of ten Sunday mornings, Black and I were not home. We are generally still on the road. When Black arrived at the residence, he observed a few peculiar things. The first was that no one was out working. The second was that an unusual vehicle was parked outside the guesthouse. The third red flag was the guest house's garage being closed. All of the groundskeeping tools—lawn mowers, Weed Eaters, rakes, and shovels—were kept in the garage, which was usually open.

Black knocked on the front door, but nobody answered. When he went around the back, he was unable to see inside. The window was covered with a black plastic substance.

He went over to the main house and eventually located Leo. They exchanged words. Black was curious as to why no one was outside and who had parked their car at the guesthouse. He could not get a straight answer from him. Leo was evasive. He kept changing the subject. At this moment, Black called and informed me that we had a problem.

"Nobody was working when I got here," he stated. "And I think they've got people staying there too."

I knew what was going on, and I was furious. These Chicos assumed I was out of town and decided to throw themselves a party. Not only were they not working, but they had brought strangers into my home and were doing who knows what. I immediately requested that Black come pick me up.

The garage door had been opened by the time we returned. I took my revolver, instructed Black to wait outside, and stormed into the house. As I walked down the hallway, I could hear sounds coming from within the bedroom. I could smell smoke, but it wasn't cannabis. I didn't identify the fragrance. I called out, but nobody responded. I then entered the room.

Because of the taped-off windows, it was dark inside. But I noticed there was a young woman I didn't know. She was naked above the waist. Then I felt someone reach out and grab me from behind.

I whirled around and whacked the person who had just touched me with the revolver. Then I hit him again. I must have hit him with the corner of it, because blood was streaming everywhere. That's when I discovered it was Leo. He was severely split.

The young woman began screaming, and as I returned my gaze, I noticed she was accompanied by a young child. Then I heard two more voices coming down the corridor. It was another couple who had a child as well. Except for Leo, I didn't recognize any of these people. I began waving the rifle about and telling them everyone to get out of the house. They accomplished this in a hurry.

When I walked outside, Black was fighting with Jonathan. Jonathan had arrived and attempted to enter the residence after hearing the disturbance. Of course, Black wouldn't allow it to happen, and blows were thrown.

I cursed everyone out and made them leave. The entire thing occurred in less than ten minutes. The next day, after my rage had calmed, I had Black contact Jonathan and Leo to resolve the situation. I was still outraged about what they had done, but cracking open Leo's dome was an accident. It didn't have to happen that way.

I'm not sure what Jonathan said to Black when he called. But he certainly didn't inform him that he had already gone to the police. Or that he told them that Black and I had carried him back into the house and battered him with the pistol for another ten minutes.

Three days later, Deputy Grier was sneaking outside my fence, waiting for me. Two weeks later, twenty US Marshals descended on the studio house.

After three weeks in the hole, I was now on home arrest. I felt paranoid. I knew they were watching my every move with the GPS ankle monitor, but could the device be recording my conversations? My lawyer stated it was impossible, but I wasn't convinced. This case was complete garbage, but it made me distrustful of everything. Especially the bit involving the US Marshals. Anything related to the feds immediately put me on high alert.

One of the first things I recall happening while I was under house arrest was Meek attacking Drake on Twitter. That puzzled me. Drake and I had a long-standing bond, and as far as I knew, so did Meek. They'd made a smash hit together a few years ago called "Amen," and Meek had recently featured Drake on a song called "R.I.C.O." that was shaping up to be one of the album's biggest singles. For whatever reason, Meek was now aiming for Drake's throat.

Meek publicly accused Drake of offending him by using a ghostwriter on "R.I.C.O." I didn't believe it. I reasoned that one of two things was happening. Either Meek was letting his nuts dangle and believed he had the juice to challenge Drake for the title, or this was about something else. I had an idea what that something else may be. Meek and Drake shared deep feelings for the same woman. Nicki Minaj.

Nicki and I had worked together on various occasions throughout the years, and when she and Meek started dating, she would spend a lot of time at my place. They were there the night before the Feds arrived. Nicki was cool. I have nothing against her. But this was a new friendship, and when it came down to it, I knew Nicki would never go against Wayne and Drake. The Young Money team spirit was as strong as MMG's was. I didn't want Meek's pillow chat to be used against him. I told him to be cautious.

But Lil Fish was in love and didn't want to hear it from me. So I took a step back and let the scenario unfold naturally. It did not go well for Meek. Drake was battle-tested and war-ready, and he responded with two devastating disses. By the time Meek could come up with one of his own, the prevailing impression was that this feud was done and not even close.

Behind the scenes, I did my best to keep things under control. I chatted with Drake's huge friend, J. Prince, and we were on the same page. There was nothing except affection and mutual respect. But when I contacted Birdman, Drake's label boss, I was met with apathy and dismissal. His guy was winning this war; why should he care about mine?

At that time, I began to seriously question my relationship with Birdman. Wayne phoned me from Rikers Island, and I knew he wasn't backed by Stunna. Wayne was now suing him for over $50 million in unpaid advances and album royalties. Meanwhile, Khaled had just broken out of his deal with Cash Money after years of having to pay producers out of pocket because Birdman refused to cut the check. T-Mix, the Suave House producer I used to collaborate with in Greg Street's basement, went on to produce for Cash Money after Mannie Fresh departed the label. He was never properly credited or compensated for his work.

This was a dishonourable man. For a long time, I ignored it because I admired Birdman and respected his achievements in the game. We had already recorded an entire album together. But after he showed his hand in the Meek and Drake scenario, all of my respect for him vanished.

I wanted to go to war for Meek, but I didn't see the point in ruining my friendship with Drake. I had a feeling the two of them were going to make up shortly regardless. But I wanted to make it clear that I supported Lil Fish, which I did. So I went for Birdman instead.

I wouldn't know for another month if I'd be able to travel for work while under house arrest, and I was becoming a bit insane. So I locked myself in the studio and began working on my new album, Black Market.

Even if I had permission to travel, I was aware that there would be numerous restrictions. I wouldn't be able to effectively promote a record. Black Market was also my final contractual obligation with Def Jam, and I had a sense they wouldn't be laying out the red carpet for my next album. We had a long history together, but our partnership had come to an end. They knew I'd leave after this one.

I needed to find a way to make this record unique. Hood Billionaire had its moments, but it lacked the connection with fans that Teflon Don, Rich Forever, and God Forgives, I Don't had. I needed to right the ship with Black Market as I prepared for major label free agency.

I remembered Teflon Don, which was released in 2010. How I teased the album with The Albert Anastasia EP initially, and the excitement it sparked when listeners heard "B.M.F." and "MC Hammer." I was planning to do it again. The Black Market required a forerunner. That predecessor became Black Dollar.

Black Dollar was born out of a period of seclusion. I was not travelling at the time. I wasn't at the clubs. I was not smoking. I was at home. Those circumstances revealed a different side of myself. Less boldness equals more insight. I didn't make a conscious effort to create a distinct type of album. It's just what was flowing out of me at the moment. Even the beats I chose were different.

The spirit of the Black Dollar passed over to the Black Market. I eventually gained permission to travel for domestic gigs and appearances, but I was fully aware that this album could be my last as a free man. If it was, what did I want to say? What did I want my legacy to be like? That was the driving force behind songs like "Foreclosures" and "Free Enterprise."

Two months after the release of Black Market, a Fayette County grand jury formally indicted me and Black on twelve felony charges stemming from the incident at my estate: two counts of kidnapping, seven counts of aggravated assault, and three counts of possessing a firearm while committing a felony. That's when the gravity of my situation began to seep in. I only had to be convicted of one of these offences to receive a life sentence.

Consider the charges I had pending. I was startled to receive an invitation to the White House a few weeks after being indicted. President Barack Obama invited a dozen artists to Washington, DC, for a roundtable discussion on criminal justice reform and My Brother's Keeper, his project to help young black brothers achieve their full potential. I felt honoured to be a part of a group that includes Khaled, Wale, Busta Rhymes, Chance the Rapper, Nicki Minaj, Pusha T, J. Cole, John Legend, Ludacris, Alicia Keys, and Janelle Monae.

Aside from my legal troubles, meeting Obama came at the best time. Wayne Parker was awarded executive clemency by Obama two weeks earlier. Obama commuted the sentences of hundreds of nonviolent drug prisoners, and Wayne was released after seventeen years in prison. Given that I was the last person to see Wayne before the authorities apprehended him, it only seemed to make sense that I would be the first person he saw when he was released in a few months. I was going to pick him up and drive him directly to the Mercedes-Benz showroom. I wanted my big friend to be living the same way he was when he got in. I owed Obama a debt of gratitude, and I wanted to thank him personally. I also wanted to see what he could do for Kano. However, Kano's case was slightly more complicated.

Obama was discussing the ability of artists to have a profound impact on young people. What stayed with me was when he discussed all of his intentions for after his presidency. This was not about getting a bunch of celebrities to support him so he could earn some votes for his next reelection. He was truly concerned about making a difference. I respected that. He inspired me to step up my efforts to accomplish the same.

Obama was spouting some serious trash, but my mind began to wander. This was so strange. It had been ten years since I wrote the song "White House" for Port of Miami, and now I was in the actual White House, meeting with the President of the United States. I felt pleased with myself. I had come a long way.

BEEP, BEEP, BEEP!

My walk down memory lane had just been interrupted by the sound of my ankle monitor alerting me that it needed to be charged. I extended my leg beneath the desk, intending to cover the sound. But everyone in the room heard the shit go off. Secret Service agents began surrounding the room, trying to find out where the sound was coming from. Before the meeting, we were all required to check our cell phones to ensure that no one had anything beeping on them.

BEEP! BEEP! Fuck.

When it went off for the second time, all eyes turned to me. Khaled's brow was covered in beads of sweat once again. Before I could realise what was going on, the ankle monitor lost its mind.

BEEP! BEEP! BEEP! BEEP! BEEP! BEEP!

"What is that noise?" Obama finally asked. He was the first to say something.

I raised one hand and pointed it at my ankle.

"My apologies, everyone," I said.

"Oh, you scared me there, Rick," Obama said. "I thought this place was gonna blow!"

Everybody laughed at that one. But I was also shaken up. Before my daydream was cut short, I was reflecting on where I was when I created "White House." How I still hadn't spent a dime of my Def Jam money and was in the studio between tour dates attempting to create the best album I could. How I was terrified of having fifteen minutes of glory and then returning to being a nobody. But I persevered and survived the storms. My fifteen minutes had now been going for ten years.

But the alarm from my ankle monitor pulled me back to reality. It reminded me of my current circumstances. I was on the verge of losing everything I'd accomplished thus far. And my fate would be considerably worse than simply going back to being broke. I could be heading for the chain gang.

Chapter 19

I've replayed the night of December 7, 2017, in my thoughts numerous times. I do it to find answers. To determine what I missed or what may have been done. I never find that clarity. All I can find are the boring details.

That night was the first time I ever used an Uber. I was scheduled to perform at Miami Beach's Rockwell club, but the van blew a tire on the way there. Short Legs stayed with the van and waited for AAA, while Black called us an Uber. It was as if I didn't know what Twitter was. It's difficult to keep up with all of the stuff.

It was Art Basel week, so the city was a little more crowded than usual, but for the most part, it was a normal night. We got to the club, gave the people what they came for, picked up the rear end, and left around 4:00 a.m. I had an event at Checkers the next day, so as soon as we came back, I lit a joint and fell asleep. When I try to think of something unusual, all I can come up with is that Black was standing in a different part of the club than he typically was.

Black would always come into my room at 8:00 a.m. to administer my medication. But he did not arrive that morning. I contacted his phone around 8:30, but he did not respond. When I walked into his bedroom, he was not there. I looked outside, but all of the cars were there. Perhaps he grabbed an Uber to meet up with a hoe late at night.

I contacted Short Legs and asked him to stop and get me a pair of Air Forces before coming to the house. The chain of command for stuff like that normally ran from me to Black to Short, so Short realised immediately quickly something was wrong.

"Okay, no problem," he said. "Everything straight?"

"I believe so. Do you talk to Black? "He's not answering his phone."

"Nah, I ain't heard from the dog yet."

Short arrived at the house with the sneakers at 10:30. We had to leave to head to Checkers soon, and there had been no word from Black. We called Kane.

"You talk to Black?"

"Not since last night."

This was really unlike Black. If it had been Slab, I would not have been concerned until he was gone for a month. That is Slab. But Black didn't do anything like this. Especially when we had somewhere to go.

Short suspected Black had gotten drunk and passed out by the lake, so he decided to bike around the area to see if he could find him. But, just before leaving, he discovered some garments on the floor of one of the bedrooms. Nobody was staying in that room, which Short had just straightened out the day before.

The room was vacant, although someone had been present. Short went to check the bathroom and discovered vomit in and around the toilet. When he opened the shower curtain, he found him. Black was spread out in the tub.

"Man, are you sleeping in the bathtub?! "Come on, bro, we have to go!"

Black did not respond, and when Short grasped his leg to wake him up, he noticed it was chilly. He placed his hand underneath his nose. Black was not breathing.

Short dashed downstairs as I was getting ready to leave with my two security guards, Tank and Jerry.

"Dog upstairs!" Short shouted. I knew there was something wrong. I don't recall hearing Short raise his voice like that before.

"What do you mean?"

"Black's upstairs! "He's not right!"

Short dialled 911, and we all went upstairs. The operator informed him that an ambulance was on its way and to begin administering chest compressions. Short did them until he grew exhausted, at which point Jerry stepped in. Jerry is much bigger than Short, so we assumed he would be more effective. Nothing.

When the paramedics arrived, they forced everyone out of the room. I was still completely in denial about what was happening. I was sure they'd come out in a few minutes with Black on a stretcher. He'd give us a thumbs up, and we'd all go to the hospital to figure out what had happened.

But they were not taking Black to the hospital. That reality dawned on me when the paramedics emerged from the bathroom and Black was not on the gurney. One of them went outside to the ambulance and returned with a body bag.

"What are you all doing?! "Ain't you going to revive him?"

"We apologise. "He's gone."

Everything after that is a blur. I was shocked. Despite the fact that he had just discovered the death of his best buddy, Short Legs maintained his composure and attempted to control the situation. He was attempting to keep something from coming out. He knew that as soon as it happened, there would be complete mayhem. But it was too late for that. Everybody's phones blew up. The first blacks. Then ours. My sister had contacted D'vante, Black's son, and he had called Kane and Quise, who arrived at the house a few minutes later. I don't even want to know how they got past the gates since at that point, some unfortunate security person may have been killed attempting to stop them from entering. When they arrived at the house, the cops were also trying to keep them out. It's a marvel they didn't get harmed too. Quise looked like he was about to pass out. I was really close.

The medical examiner ruled that Black died of heart illness at the age of forty-five. His arteries were blocked. I'm not sure how much Black knew about his cholesterol or other health issues, but I know he wouldn't have told me about them regardless. Black had become seriously ill a few years prior, but he kept it a secret until Short Legs discovered him and had to transport him to the hospital for emergency surgery. This is how Black was. He looked after a lot of people, but he refused to allow anyone to look after him. He did not want to be a burden.

I know Black drank Red Bulls religiously. Every time we went to the store, he would come out with two Red Bulls, a Snickers bar, a packet of sunflower seeds, and some Backwoods. So Black's behaviours were not the healthiest. But neither had I. That terrified me.

But why the hell was Black in the bathtub? I'd never seen him in that room. He always slept in his room or on the couch below.

We'll never know for certain, but Short Legs could have solved the mystery. As I already stated, if Black knew he was unwell, he would not have told me. Our rooms were adjacent to each other, so I would have heard if he was throwing up or gasping for air. Short assumed Black had gone across the hall because he didn't want me to hear what he was going through. That devastated my heart, but I believe Short was correct.

It wasn't the first time I had lost a close buddy. In 2010, my friend P-Nut was killed in a home invasion. Two shooters waited for him outside his Miramar home as he returned from a Christmas celebration. He gave up the money, but it wasn't sufficient. He was shot dead in front of his wife and three sons.

P-Nut was one of my best friends, yet it was always clear that he prioritises his family. Regardless of what was going on with me, P-Nut would drop Raymond, Raynard, and Raymelle off at school and Tameka off at work every morning. He planned to pick them all up in the afternoon. He might catch up with me later, but at the end of the night, he was going home to them. They arrived first.

Like Nut, Black was a proud father of three. D'vante, Nadaja, and Khaniyah were undoubtedly the apple of his eye. All he did was for them. But, unlike P-Nut, Black never truly left my side. He was the first person I saw each morning. He'd come upstairs to wake me up, and then we'd start the day together. Whatever I got into, Black would be right there with me. He was my shadow.

Throughout our legal proceedings, the prosecutor always referred to Black as my bodyguard. I did not like that. Black would be the first to take buck shots at any threat that came my way, and he had done it countless times before. But he was far more than hired muscle. It didn't feel right to call him my bodyguard.

No amount of money could purchase Black's allegiance to me. Our bond existed before I hired him. Our friendship predates that by fifteen years. He was my true right hand. So I wasn't just going to miss him like I did P-Nut. I needed black. I didn't know how to live without him.

But the Lord has blessed me with many wonderful friends. After Black died, everyone moved up to fill the vacuum he had left in all of us. I was fortunate to have Tomcat and Short Legs with me when I experienced another seizure three months later.

This one was different. I had gotten a cold the day before and had a severe cough. I had been taking DayQuil and applying Vicks VapoRub all day. When I went to bed that night, I had a seizure. But I did not come out of it as I usually do. My breathing was all messed up. At about 3:30 a.m., the female I was with went downstairs and informed Tomcat that I had shit myself and was foaming at the mouth.

After a few minutes, I was able to get out of bed. I was still not breathing well, so I went into the shower to clean off and attempt to get myself together. When the ambulances and police arrived, I instructed Tomcat to turn them away. I had been through this before. I'd be straightforward. But then I started coughing up blood while showering. That had never occurred before.

At that point, Tomcat advised me to go to the hospital. Short Legs arrived and transported me to the nearest hospital, where physicians discovered I had aspiration pneumonia. Something had gotten into my lungs during the seizure and developed an infection. I was sedated and connected to a breathing machine.

I had been hospitalised for something similar a year previously. We kept it quiet and it never hit the headlines, but it was serious. What occurred was that I took my plea deal in April and hit the road hard. As usual, spending a lot of time on the road caused me to get less sleep and damaged my immune system. You can guess what came next. I suffered a seizure while flying home from Europe. I was in the hospital for one week.

This time, physicians were more concerned. Because I had just returned from playing in Nairobi, Kenya. They were concerned that I had brought back some sort of infection from Africa and wanted to put me under quarantine.

When my mother arrived at the hospital, she handled the situation as she always does. She didn't trust this facility to handle me correctly, so she transported me to Memorial Regional Hospital in Hollywood, where they drained my lungs with a tube and gave me medicines. TMZ stated that I was hooked up to an ECMO machine, but it was never that serious. I'm no expert, but according to what I've heard, being put on ECMO is a terrible omen.

So much has transpired since I began writing this book. I lost Black Bo and came dangerously close to death. Another buddy of mine, Nipsey Hussle, was slain in the town he was attempting to rehabilitate. The footage of his death, as well as how it was disseminated to the rest of the world, deeply saddened me. I've seen niggas die before. I understand what rigour mortis looks like. And I've probably crossed paths with a few rats in my day, including Eric Holder. But the thought of such an honourable brother as Nipsey going down like that and having that be his final image made me sick. If that low-life rat believed that going to the mad house and allowing the cops to come for him would be the end of the story, he was quite incorrect.

A thirty-one-year-old man named Lavel Mucherson was fatally shot a few days ago near 37th Avenue and 207th Street, only one red light away from the old Matchbox housing. They also hit his seven-year-old kid, who was in the car with him. When the authorities opened the truck to find the dead, they discovered a semi-automatic rifle and two handguns inside. I didn't know the young man, but I did know his mother. She was great friends with Jabbar's baby mother. I'm praying for her and her family.

The city can rename Carol City Miami Gardens or anything they want, but it won't change the way of life out here. When I started writing this, I wanted to portray a picture of a specific environment at a particular period. However, everything I'm telling you about is still happening right now. That is why they name it Murder Gardens.

I'm not afraid of death, but I am afraid of unfinished business. When my father died, the most difficult aspect was not that he was gone. He hadn't been in my life for a while. The hardest thing was dealing with my regrets from when he was alive. There were numerous unspoken words between us.

Briana, a wonderful woman, recently made me a parent again. Twice. Our daughter is two years old, and our boy is 10 months old.

If something were to happen to me, I want Toie, Will, Berkeley, and Billion to know who their father is. And I want them to hear it directly from me. Both excellent and awful. I simply don't want to leave any words unanswered.

These are a few of the reasons I wanted to share my story. I wanted to rip back the veil on my life and give niggas some game while I still had the opportunity. However, there are many topics that I will never be able to properly describe or understand. How is it possible that a former correctional officer has ties to the most successful hustlers in Carol City history? How is it that after all of these street fights and shootings, I can still move comfortably? How come I live the way I do when just one of my albums has gone platinum?

50 Cent has sold over 30 million records. How come, while he was declaring bankruptcy and selling Mike Tyson's old castle for peanuts, I was racing across the former Holyfield estate on one of my four horses? Do you have any clue what it costs to care for four horses? I pay more for hay and horseshoes than these rap niggas do for their kids. Tell me: how is that possible?

I can't tell you. Forgive me for that. I hope everybody who has read this book has read between the lines. There's a lot being said here that isn't in black print.

When I began working on my tenth album, Port of Miami 2, I wondered if the experience would provide me with a sense of closure. There is a sense of things coming full circle. I hoped that authoring this book would achieve the same result. However, it seemed more like striking the reset button. It brought back all of my feelings from the moment. The hunger. The pain. The courage. The aggressive behaviour. It started a fire within me. My passion for music is genuine, and I am confident that I will continue to improve.

So, this is not the end. Like Nipsey Hussle would say, "The Marathon Continues." But how do you wrap up a story that isn't over? How do you end a book when there are still chapters left? The majority of autobiographies I've read were written by folks who were past their prime. As much as I adore my horses, I'm not prepared to ride off into the sunset.

What if I don't finish this memoir and my most memorable memories are still to come? God willing, that will be the case.

I had to consider the question for a long time. I disregarded deadlines because I didn't want to miss the next hurricane. But there will always be another storm. I have to come to terms with telling my story as it is. And I made peace with it. Because the truth is that the stories I tell do not define me as a boss. It's the ones that I don't.

Made in the USA
Monee, IL
09 October 2024

67580887R00085